feed your
family for
£20 a week

I'd like to dedicate this book to two amazing women who are sadly no longer with us. To my nana who was everything a loving grandmother should be and more besides. I don't ever remember hearing her raise her voice, her home was a cosy place where we were loved and fed very well! And to my mum, taken from us too soon. I wish you'd had a chance to stick around longer!

You are loved and missed every day
xx

feed your family for £20 a week

Lorna Cooper

SEVEN DIALS

Hi folks,

My name is Lorna and five years ago I set up the Facebook community Feed Your Family for £20 a Week. I started it because I saw so many young families struggling in the current economic climate and wanted to help them to feed their families good, home-cooked food on a budget.

I'm a mother of three and stepmother of two. With such a busy house and so many mouths to feed, I know how hard it is to put good, hearty food on the table without breaking the bank. Over the years, I've learnt all the tips and tricks – minimising waste, bulking out meals, using up leftovers, shopping around and baking (rather than buying) all our treats.

Feeding your family for £20 a week isn't about handing someone two tenners for a week's shopping. It's about shopping smart, cooking from scratch, batch cooking, making the most of your freezer, adapting recipes to use what you have and learning to love your leftovers.

To get you started, there is an eight-week meal plan to feed your family of four (pages 16–23) and a shopping list that will cost you £160 in total. I know this sounds like a large investment, but not only will you have eight weeks' worth of lovely meals, you will also have the building blocks to continue this plan for ever.

Each recipe is full of flavour, easy to follow and many are ready in minutes. So, let's get stuck in and learn how to meal plan, budget and cook three meals a day, seven days a week for just £20. I promise you will never look back!

XX Lorna XX

CONTENTS

HOW TO FEED YOUR FAMILY FOR £20:

HOW IT ALL BEGAN

I would say that for most households the biggest obstacles to eating well are lack of time and money. There are still so many people who believe that it is cheaper and easier to buy pizzas, chicken nuggets and fishfingers rather than make them, and I can certainly relate to that.

I grew up in Paisley with my mum, dad and big sister. Dad was a college lecturer by day and a bricklayer after hours. Mum was the heart of the house. Life was simple and perfect. Then when I was ten, my mum was diagnosed with breast cancer and died just as I turned eleven. My dad remarried eighteen months later, and we all moved to Erskine.

Mum had been everything to all of us and we found it hard to adjust to her being gone and then having a stepmother. Eventually, when I turned 14 and my sister 18, Dad bought a house down the road for me and my sister to live in. I suppose that's when I first began thinking about food and money. I had to fend for, feed myself and run the house.

Dad would check in on us often and take us food shopping but there was no logic to what we threw in the trolley and certainly no attempt at creating any kind of coherent meal. At 16, I met my first husband. Dad wasn't happy I had a boyfriend and so, in the end, I left home. That's when reality hit – we were completely broke, on £44 a week in benefit money, and I had to run the house and feed and clothe us on that. My husband had taken over the tenancy on his dad's council house, so we had a roof over our heads, but the change for me was a big one and I realised I would have to improvise fast.

I'd go to the butcher to buy a full lorne of sausage for £2 and then I'd go to a bargain supermarket to buy ten loaves for 25p each. My final stop would be the local farm to stock up on vegetables as they were cheaper there. I'd get a sack of potatoes for £3 and a large tray of eggs and then that was it, the budget was gone. Our menu was the same most days: toast and sausage for breakfast, scrambled egg on toast for lunch and sausage and chips for dinner.

When I had my children – a girl first, then a boy sixteen months later – I realised I had to step it up with more nutritious recipes, so I called my nana to ask for her recipes and started being more creative with budgets and ingredients. Once my son was a few months old, I started working again so things eased slightly financially, but five months after I had my third child, I was diagnosed with a heart condition. My lungs were full of liquid and my heart was double the size it should be. I was sent straight to A&E and was in hospital for a week, before being put on the waiting list for a biventricular pacemaker. I was the first person in Scotland to get one!

These health issues made me look seriously at how I ate and what cooking really meant. I began to enjoy cooking from scratch and experimented with what I served my family. I put a system in place to stop waste and mindless buying, concentrating on things that would actually make a proper meal. I would plan out each week and write my shopping list at home so I could check the cupboards to make sure I wasn't buying things we already had. I involved my kids with the meal planning too, which made them less fussy eaters.

My heart condition made me take stock in more ways than one, and after a time, I realised my husband and I had outgrown each other. I met my current partner John through a support group as we have the same heart condition. We settled into life as a couple and all was well until I slipped a disc. I didn't qualify for sick pay and suddenly money was mega-tight once again. This time I was prepared: I went back to my strict planning and gave myself a budget of £20 a week to feed all of us. That's when the FYF community was born.

One afternoon, I was mindlessly scrolling through a Facebook group when someone asked if they could use double cream if the use-by date was the previous day. This question opened up a whole debate about food in general and before I knew it, I was dishing out all sorts of advice: recipes, money-saving tips, budgeting, what is and isn't good for you, even how long defrosted chicken can stay in the fridge before you need to use it! Someone suggested I start a food-specific Facebook page to help answer questions about meal planning and saving money and, well, here we are – all these likes later.

Now, over half a million people have joined my Feed Your Family Facebook community and they've learnt how to cook smart with minimum fuss and maximum flavour – all for just £20 A WEEK! And now, I want to show you how, too.

LORNA'S TOP 10 MONEY SAVING TIPS

1. FREEZER SHOPS

When I was really skint, Dad would come down and take me to the freezer shop so I could stock up on frozen meat. Chicken breasts and stewing beef were often on offer and I would bulk-buy and fill up my freezer, without having to worry about sell-by dates. Remember, running an empty freezer is more expensive than running a full one. Also, I often get leaflets through my door with all the latest offers: £2 off a £25 shop, £5 off when you spend £50, etc. I always save them in my purse, so make sure you do the same!

2. MAKE YOUR FRESH INGREDIENTS LAST

Blanching and then freezing your veg is a great way to get the best from fresh veg. If you buy reduced veg, or find some that's bendy or sprouting, throw it in hot water for a minute, then plunge straight into cold water before allowing to dry. Freeze flat on a baking tray so that they don't freeze in a clump then transfer to a freezer bag. If you're freezing lots of storage bags then put a bit of oil on the outside of each bag as it stops the bags from sticking together once frozen.

3. TWO FOR ONE

People argue they don't have time to batch cook and don't want to spend their whole Sunday in the kitchen cooking endless meals. I hear you, believe me! My mantra is double up – if you're making a lasagne, make two, it takes you no more time. One for dinner and one for the freezer is my motto.

4. PLANNING IS KEY

Make your shopping list at home and never assume you need something without checking. Think about your shop in terms of ingredients and what you'll make with them, not just food for food's sake.

5. BULK-BUY

Wherever possible buy in bulk! If you see a really good deal buy as much as you can afford (and are able to store). If you can't afford to buy something in bulk, consider grouping together with family or friends.

6. SHOP AROUND

One of the biggest mistakes people make is just going to one shop for everything. Shopping around may be less convenient, but it can, and does, make a huge difference to your budget. If you can't get to lots of different shops remember to look at the basics options in the supermarket. These are often as good as the branded items. Bargain stores are also a fantastic place to find store cupboard items like stock cubes, crushed garlic and tinned tomatoes at reduced prices.

7. KNOW WHERE TO LOOK

Herbs and spices are much cheaper from Asian supermarkets than they are from the chain supermarkets. If there isn't one near you then often the world food aisle in the supermarket is cheaper than buying the small jars.

8. GROW YOUR OWN

You don't always need to buy herbs, as you can grow many yourself without needing a large space to do so – a windowsill or small planter is ideal. Some areas have community herb gardens where you can pop along and take a cutting. Or ask your friends, family or neighbours who may already grow their own and be happy to help you get started! You can easily dry your home-grown herbs as well as using them fresh. You'll save a small fortune.

9. BULK OUT

By bulking out meat with vegetables, porridge oats and various pulses you can save money without affecting the quantity or quality of the food you serve up to your family. I regularly bulk out my meat in this way and have had no complaints!

10. LOVE YOUR LEFTOVERS

Do you routinely find yourself scraping leftovers into the bin because you don't think they're worth saving? Many of my recipes use leftover bits and pieces, so save them all! You can also freeze your leftovers – too much soup or pasta? Freeze it for another time. Having leftovers doesn't have to mean eating the same thing the next day.

ADAPTING RECIPES

This book is for all of you who want to feed your family for £20 a week, whether through necessity or choice. However, we all have likes and dislikes. Maybe you're just here for the recipes and aren't particularly bothered about the budget, or maybe your family has allergies or medical conditions. All my recipes can be adapted to suit budgets, dietary needs and taste. I use a lot of frozen food because when you're on a tight budget it is generally cheaper and it's easier to portion out with less waste (which is more likely to happen if you have to eat the same vegetables four days in a row!). But if you'd prefer, you can use fresh vegetables in their place as well as more expensive cuts of meat than the ones I've suggested. I have also included in some recipes 'Feelin' Fancy' add-ons – suggestions for if you're a bit flush or want something that extra bit special!

One of the simplest ways to reduce your shopping bill is to adapt the recipes you use the most. If a recipe calls for organic crushed garlic, you don't have to rush out and blow your budget if you have another kind of garlic, whether granules, powder or fresh. I don't care what anyone says, garlic is garlic! The same goes for chillies, basil, tarragon – loads of fresh ingredients can be subbed for dried. Here's a handy chart to help you.

FRESH TO DRIED

HERB	FRESH	DRIED
BASIL	2 tsp	1 tsp
BAY LEAF	1 leaf	2 leaves
CINNAMON	1 stick	½ tsp
DILL	3 tsp	1 tsp
GARLIC	1 clove (½ tsp crushed)	⅛ tsp
GINGER	2cm (1 tbsp crushed)	½ tsp
MARJORAM	3 tsp	1 tsp
ONION	1 medium	1 tsp
OREGANO	3 tsp	1 tsp
PARSLEY	2 tsp	1 tsp
ROSEMARY	3 tsp	1 tsp
SAGE	2 tsp	1 tsp
TARRAGON	3 tsp	1 tsp
THYME	3 tsp	1 tsp

You can also be flexible with the meat and veg in your recipe. If you don't like beef, try a chicken lasagne. If you find pork or turkey mince in the reduced aisle, use them like you would beef mince. Got burgers or sausages you don't fancy? Break them up and use them as mince. Leftover bolognese makes an amazing cottage pie!

When I find a new recipe I like the look of, I usually make it as per the method the first time round (bar the organic garlic!), and then I start to think 'How can I add more veg?' or 'How can I make this recipe easier and cheaper?' Often I think 'Can I make this a one-pot meal?' because like most mums, I'm always in a rush! In this busy day and age, adapting recipes to make them quicker, easier and cheaper is something I enjoy and, luckily for me, I have you guys to share my creations with.

So, play about with food and flavours, don't be daunted by posh recipes and if you're stuck give me a shout on the blog and I'll do my best to help.

SO LET'S GET STARTED!

This shopping list will get you through the 8 week plan on the following pages. Shopping around is key to getting these prices and if you really want to stick to the budget, you'll have to freeze portions and use your leftovers as I've suggested. You'll also need to make the homemade versions of ingredients as listed in each recipe (don't worry, I've suggested alternatives for those of you who are just here for the recipes!), all of which are found in the Basics section. It may seem difficult at times, but it's worth the legwork and if you stick to this plan like I do, you'll never look back!

SHOPPING LIST

SUPERMARKET

4kg carrots	96p
1kg parsnips	66p
Celery sticks	50p
6kg brown onions	£3
Lettuce	45p
2 x cherry tomatoes pack	£1.08
Cucumber	60p
4 pack garlic	90p
2 x 6 small banana bunches	90p
5 x lemons	92p
2 x 1kg gammon joint	£5.98
1 x 500g natural yoghurt	£1
Ham hock	£1.49
2 x 1kg long grain rice	90p
2kg red lentils	£2.30
600g broth/soup mix	80p
4 x 1kg porridge oats	£3
Pizza base mix	65p
4 x 1kg flour	£1.80
5 x 500g penne pasta	£1.45
500g spaghetti	20p
10 x noodles	£1.40
Lasagne sheets	50p
1l apple juice	55p
long life cream alternative	£1.10
12 x part-baked baguette 2-pack	£5.04
1 x bread loaf (freeze in portions)	36p
Pitta bread 6-pack	50p
2 x English muffins 4-pack	£1.20
2l vegetable oil	£2.20
800g breadcrumbs	£1
3 x 20 frozen sausages	£2.73
4 x 110g tin tuna	£2.36
212g tin pink salmon	£1.95
Tin sardines in tomato sauce	40p
8 x 400g tin chopped tomatoes	£2

4 x 400g tin baked beans	92p
2 x Casserole veg	£1
1kg chicken thighs	£1.50
4 x 30 eggs	£8
6 x puff pastry	£4
2 x 7.5kg potatoes	£8
2 x 18 slices bacon	£3.98

BUY AS NEEDED

12 pints of milk	£3.00
6 x 400g cheddar (freeze)	£10.74
2 x 500g soft spread (butter alternative)	£1.38
5 x spring onion	£4.40
3 x tubs soft cheese	£1.65
12 x tomatoes	£1.30

FREEZER SHOP

5 for £4 (£16 total)

2 x corn cob	Carrots
2 x spinach	Swede
Cauliflower	Cabbage
Broccoli	Stir fry veg
Leek	Mixed vegetables
4 x sliced peppers	650g sweetcorn
3 x peas	

5 for £15 (£36 total)

3 x 900g chicken breast fillets	500g lamb mince
	500g diced beef
2 x 1.7kg ready to roast chicken	2 x 900g white fish fillets
	3 x 500g beef steak mince

3 for £5 (£15 total)

1 x 450g pineapple	2 x 450g blueberries
2 x 550g blackberries	1 x 450g mango
2 x 600g strawberries	800g sliced apples

Voucher	-£10
Total	**£159.70**

STORE CUPBOARD

These items are all things I would expect to find in most people's cupboards. And if they're not, then they should be! But don't worry we won't use them all up, just a teaspoon here and there.

Allspice	Curry powder	Parsley
Baking powder	Dried fruit	Sage
Basil	Garlic powder	Salt & pepper
Bay leaves	Gherkins	Soy sauce
Brown sauce	Ginger	Stock cubes
Cajun spices	Honey	Sugar
Cayenne pepper	Jam	Sultanas
Celery salt	Ketchup	Syrup
Chickpeas	Mayonnaise	Thyme
Chilli powder/flakes	Mixed herbs	Tinned potatoes
Chilli sauce	Mixed nuts	Tomato purée
Chinese five spice	Mustard	Turmeric
Cinnamon	Onion powder	Vanilla essence
Coriander	Oregano	Vinegar
Cornflour	Paprika	Worcester sauce

KEY EQUIPMENT

Most of my recipes don't require much, but some things I can't do without are:

Blender

Slow cooker

Big freezer

Freezer bags

Tupperware

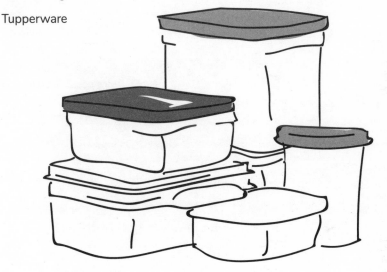

Online markets such as Facebook and Gumtree are great places to shop for kitchenware. People often buy stuff that looks nice or matches their kitchen and then only use a few times before storing and eventually selling on.

Week 1

Day	Breakfast	Lunch	Dinner
Sun	Fluffy Scotch Pancakes (page 35)	Scotch Broth (page 47)	Roast Chicken (page 88) Fondant Potatoes (page 174) Mixed Veg
Mon	Berry Blast Overnight Oats (page 26)	Pizza Pin Wheels (page 67)	Chicken & Rice Soup (page 49) Part-baked Baguette
Tue	Bircher Muesli (page 29)	Cheese Puffs (page 69)	Gnocchi (page 112)
Wed	Breakfast Sundae (page 34)	Minestrone (page 51)	Tuna Fishcakes (page 94) Simple Carrot Salad (page 61)
Thu	Baked Oats (page 30)	Slow Cooker Jacket Potatoes (page 173)	5-A-Day Sausage Pasta (page 100)
Fri	On-the-Go Breakfast Flapjacks (page 31)	Mini Crustless Quiche (page 66)	Chicken Fried Rice (page 132)
Sat	Sausage Hash (page 38)	One-Pot Noodles (page 57)	Omelette (page 171) Salad

 When you see this icon in a recipe, freeze half of your batch in portions for a meal in the coming days or weeks. It appears in the meal plan for when you'll eat those saved portions.

 When you see this, it means you'll be saving leftovers from the meal you have just cooked, to be used in a recipe later in the week or month.

Week 2

Day	Breakfast	Lunch	Dinner
Sun	Jammy Heart French Toast (page 39)	Tomato & Lentil Soup (page 56)	Hearty Beef Pie (page 80) Boiled Potatoes Peas and Corn
Mon	Good Morning Muffins (page 28)	Mini Hotpies (page 71)	Parsnip Soup (page 52) Part-baked Baguette
Tue	Porridge (page 185)	Slow Cooker Jacket Potatoes (page 173)	Chicken Jambalaya (page 122) Homemade Flatbread (page 197)
Wed	Granola & Yoghurt Popsicles (page 33)	Cheese Puffs (page 69)	Fish Traybake (page 96)
Thu	Breakfast Sundae (page 34)	❄ Chicken & Rice Soup	Cheesy Veggie Pasta (page 102)
Fri	Banana Breakfast Cookies (page 27)	❄ 5-A-Day Sausage Pasta	'Make-Your-Own Pizza' Night (page 134) Wedges (page 176) Corn on the Cob
Sat	Italian Baked Eggs (page 40)	❄ Scotch Broth	Spaghetti Bolognese (page 125)

When you see this icon, it means you'll be using leftovers you saved while cooking a meal earlier in the plan.

feelin' fancy?

I've included some add-ons throughout the book for if you're a bit flush with extra cash and feel like adding something extra special to your meal.

Week 3

Day	Breakfast	Lunch	Dinner
Sun	Loaded Breakfast Burritos (page 36)	Chicken Noodle Soup (page 54)	Roast Gammon (page 87) Root Mash (page 178) Roast Potatoes (page 177)
Mon	Spiced Granola (page 32)	Pizza Pin Wheels (page 67)	Lentil Soup (page 55) Part-baked Baguette
Tue	Berry Blast Overnight Oats (page 26)	Mini Crustless Quiche (page 66)	Sausage Pasta Bake (page 108)
Wed	On-the-Go Breakfast Flapjacks (page 31)	Scotch Broth (page 47)	Cajun Spicy Rice (page 116)
Thu	Bircher Muesli (page 29)	One-Pot Noodles (page 57)	❄ Cheesy Veggie Pasta
Fri	Banana Breakfast Cookies (page 27)	❄ Parsnip Soup	Chicken Chow Mein (page 133)
Sat	Egg MacMuffins (page 42)	❄ Tomato & Lentil Soup	Omelette (page 171) Salad

Week 4

Day	Breakfast	Lunch	Dinner
Sun	Sausage Hash (page 38)	One-Pot Noodles (page 57)	Chicken & Sweetcorn Pie (page 84) Boiled Potatoes Peas and Corn
Mon	Porridge (page 185)	Gammon Picnic Pasta (page 110)	Potato & Leek Soup (page 46) Part-baked Baguette
Tue	Breakfast Sundae (page 34)	Pizza Pin Wheels (page 67)	Honey Soy Chicken (page 126)
Wed	Good Morning Muffins	Arancini	Tuna Pasta Bake (page 111)
Thu	Bircher Muesli	❄ Lentil Soup	Slow Cooker Jacket Potatoes (page 173)
Fri	Spiced Granola	❄ Sausage Pasta Bake	Southern Fried Chicken (page 136) Salad Corn on the Cob
Sat	Quesadillas	❄ Scotch Broth	Lasagne (page 104) Sweetcorn

Week 5

Day	Breakfast	Lunch	Dinner
Sun	Fluffy Scotch Pancakes (page 35)	❄ Potato & Leek Soup	Roast Chicken (page 88) Fondant Potatoes (page 174) Mixed Veg
Mon	Berry Blast Overnight Oats (page 26)	❄ Gammon Picnic Pasta	❄ Minestrone Part-baked Baguette
Tue	Bircher Muesli (page 29)	Pizza Pin Wheels (page 67)	Chicken Hash (page 83)
Wed	Breakfast Sundae (page 34)	Scotch Broth (page 47)	Mediterranean Pasta (page 114)
Thu	Baked Oats (page 30)	Slow Cooker Jacket Potatoes (page 173)	Easy One-Pot Rice (page 117)
Fri	On-the-Go Breakfast Flapjacks (page 31)	Tomato & Lentil Soup (page 56)	Doner Style Kebab (page 148) Salad
Sat	Sausage Hash (page 38)	Mini Crustless Quiche (page 66)	Frittata (page 72) Wedges (page 176) Sweetcorn

Week 6

Day	Breakfast	Lunch	Dinner
Sun	Jammy Heart French Toast (page 39)	❄ Tomato & Lentil Soup	Steak And Sausage Pie (page 78) Boiled Potatoes Root Mash (page 178)
Mon	Good Morning Muffins (page 28)	Mini Hotpies (page 71)	Tomato Soup (page 59) Part-Baked Baguette
Tue	Porridge (page 185)	Slow Cooker Jacket Potatoes (page 173)	Spicy Salmon Fishcakes (page 94) Simple Mint Salad (page 59)
Wed	Granola & Yoghurt Popsicles (page 33)	Cheese Puffs (page 69)	Easy-Peasy Pasta (page 105)
Thu	Breakfast Sundae (page 34)	Minestrone (page 51)	Keema Curry (page 123)
Fri	Banana Breakfast Cookies (page 27)	❄ Mediterranean Pasta	Crispy Chicken Nuggets (page 138) Twice-Cooked Chips (page 175) Strawberry Milkshake
Sat	Italian Baked Eggs (page 40)	Mini Hotpies (page 71)	Cheesy Lentil Bake (page 73)

Week 7

Day	Breakfast	Lunch	Dinner
Sun	Loaded Breakfast Burritos (page 36)	❄ Chicken Noodle Soup	Roast Gammon (page 87) Root Mash (page 178) Roast Potatoes (page 177)
Mon	Spiced Granola (page 32)	❄ Minestrone	French Onion Soup (page 53) Part-baked Baguette
Tue	Berry Blast Overnight Oats (page 26)	Mini Crustless Quiche (page 66)	Creamy Cajun Chicken Pasta (page 106)
Wed	On-the-Go Breakfast Flapjacks (page 31)	❄ Scotch Broth	Colcannon (page 74)
Thu	Bircher Muesli (page 29)	❄ Easy-Peasy Pasta	Fish Pie (page 93)
Fri	Banana Breakfast Cookies (page 27)	❄ Tomato Soup	Crispy Chilli Chicken (page 140)
Sat	Egg MacMuffins (page 42)	❄ Tuna Pasta Bake	Frittata (page 72) Salad

Week 8

Day	Breakfast	Lunch	Dinner
Sun	Sausage Hash (page 38)	❄ Chicken Noodle Soup	Sausage Meatloaf and Gravy (page 90) Mashed Potatoes Carrots
Mon	Porridge (page 185)	Cheese Puffs (page 69)	Pea & Ham Soup (page 50) Part-baked Baguette
Tue	Breakfast Sundae (page 34)	Mini Hotpies (page 71)	Bacon, Cheese & Veg Hotpot (page 92)
Wed	Good Morning Muffins (page 28)	❄ Creamy Cajun Chicken Pasta	Hawaiian Fried Rice (page 118)
Thu	Bircher Muesli (page 29)	❄ French Onion Soup	Caramelised Onion and Sausage Stew (page 91) Mashed Potatoes
Fri	Spiced Granola (page 32)	Bacon & Cheese Turnovers (page 68)	Fish & Chips with Mushy Peas (page 144)
Sat	Quesadillas (page 41)	❄ Pea & Ham Soup	Cottage Pie (page 82) Cabbage Peas

BREAKFAST

BERRY BLAST OVERNIGHT OATS

In the summer months, I tend to replace my morning porridge with a bowl of overnight oats. All the prep is done the night before, meaning you can eat on the go the next morning making it perfect for the school run or commute. Another option is to pop it in the microwave in the morning and enjoy the warm oaty goodness without the hassle of making porridge when you're still bleary-eyed!

Serves 1

125ml milk
120g yoghurt (page 188)
90g porridge oats

50g frozen fruit
½ tsp vanilla essence (optional)
½ tsp honey (optional)

Combine the milk and yoghurt, giving it a good stir. You can flavour the mix with vanilla essence or honey if you like, or leave it plain and let your fruit do all the work.

Layer the oats, yoghurt mix and fruit in a glass jar or plastic container

Cover and then pop in the fridge overnight.

This recipe makes an individual adult portion – for two adults and two kids, just triple the ingredients.

BANANA BREAKFAST COOKIES

These are absolutely delicious, and great to grab-and-go. I love to do a double batch as they freeze really well and can be defrosted overnight in the fridge. That way, I always have them at the ready for those rushed school mornings!

Serves 4

2 large bananas
80g porridge oats

50g chopped up chocolate, chocolate chips or raisins (or a combination of chocolate and raisins)

Preheat the oven to 180°C/Fan 160°C/Gas 4 and line a baking tray, ready for your cookies.

Mash the bananas really well in a large bowl. Add the oats and mix together.

Stir through the chocolate or raisins (or both if you love a chocolate-raisin combo).

Scoop out eight dollops of the mixture, placing them on the baking tray, evenly spaced.

Bake for 10–12 minutes until golden brown, then cool on a wire rack.

GOOD MORNING MUFFINS

Who doesn't love a muffin? These ones are a slightly healthier version, but are still tasty enough for the kids to think they've had cake for breakfast! Woo-hoo! I like to make 12 regular-sized muffins, but you can easily make them into 24 snack-sized mini muffins. If you like a smooth muffin, blitz the oats first for a couple of minutes in a blender or put them in a bag and attack them with a rolling pin. They also freeze really well, just make sure they have totally cooled before wrapping and freezing.

Makes 12

85g porridge oats
200g plain flour
2 tsp baking powder
½ tsp salt
75ml vegetable oil

170g Greek yoghurt
(page 188)
3 large eggs
170ml honey
½ tsp vanilla essence
75g frozen berries

Preheat the oven to 180°C/Fan 160°C/Gas 4. Put your oats in a large bowl then sieve in the dry ingredients and mix together.

In a separate bowl add all the wet ingredients, stirring until just mixed. Gently stir in the frozen berries – we don't want to mash them or the muffins will come out a weird colour!

Pour the mixture into 12 standard or 24 mini muffin cases.

Bake for 25–30 minutes if making the regular size or 15–20 minutes for the mini muffins. They're cooked when a toothpick inserted in the middle comes out clean.

Let them cool for 5 minutes before removing from the tin.

BIRCHER MUESLI

Did you know that bircher muesli was invented by a doctor who had a clinic in Switzerland? He came up with it as a healthy breakfast option for his hospital menu so we have Dr Maximilian Bircher-Benner to thank for this delicious and nutritious breakfast! Just prepare the night before and serve with fruit and cinnamon the next morning.
Just what the doctor ordered!

Serves 4

100g porridge oats
280ml milk
40ml apple juice
2 tbsp lemon juice
1–2 tbsp honey

250g plain yoghurt
(page 188)
75g apple slices,
fresh or frozen
1 tsp cinnamon,
to serve

Combine all the ingredients, except the apple and cinnamon, in a large bowl and mix well.

You can then either leave it in this bowl or split it into 4 smaller containers to make individual portions.

Cover and leave in the fridge overnight.

In the morning, top with freshly grated apple and a sprinkle of cinnamon.

BAKED OATS

This looks like a cake but it's another healthy option to prep in advance ready to be eaten on the go. I try to make a week's worth on a Sunday, wrapping them tightly or storing them in an airtight container once cooled, then keeping them in the fridge for the week ahead.

Serves 4

100g porridge oats

200g yoghurt
(page 188)

1 tbsp sugar or sweetener
(if using sweetener, you may
have to adjust the amount)

100g raspberries,
plus extra to serve

3 eggs

Preheat the oven to 200°C/Fan 180°C/Gas 6 and grease a small oven-proof dish.

Place all the ingredients, except for the eggs, into a bowl. Gently mix together, taking care not to break up the raspberries too much.

Beat the eggs in a separate bowl, then add them to the rest of the ingredients, mixing well.

Pour the mixture into the dish and bake for 30–35 minutes. It's cooked when a toothpick inserted in the middle comes out clean. Once it's cooked through, pop the dish under the grill to brown.

ON-THE-GO BREAKFAST FLAPJACKS

My son, Kyle, went through a phase of not eating breakfast and these flapjacks were the only way to get food into him in the morning. The sugar and syrup give kids an immediate burst of energy with the oats kicking in to keep them full and fuelled until lunchtime. I use home-dried fruit but you can use any kind of dried fruit you like – Kyle likes berries in his!

Makes 16

125g butter
125g sugar
2 tbsp golden syrup

250g porridge oats
50g dried fruit, chopped
(page 195)

Preheat the oven to 180°C/Fan 160°C/Gas 4 and line a 23 x 23cm baking tin with greaseproof paper.

Melt the butter, sugar and syrup in a pan over heat.

Remove the pan from the heat and stir through the oats and the dried fruit. Once combined, tip the mixture into the tin, spreading it evenly and pushing it into the corners.

Bake for 20 minutes, then allow the mixture to cool and set completely before lifting out and slicing into squares.

SPICED GRANOLA

Granola is super-expensive to buy and I always find the shop-bought ones contain something I don't like! This is a basic recipe that can be adapted very easily to your family's individual likes and dislikes. You can leave out the nuts or add in extra seeds, you can use whatever fruit you want, and you may like to add ingredients such as coconut flakes. Most oils work but they might affect the flavour. Vegetable or sunflower oil work well, as does coconut oil if you have it! Eat this as you would cereal with milk, or enjoy it with yoghurt and fruit.

Serves 20

200ml oil
200ml honey
1 tsp cinnamon
1 tsp salt

450g porridge oats
200g mixed nuts
350g dried fruit
(page 195)

Preheat the oven to 150°C/Fan 130°C/Gas 2 and line 2 large baking trays with greaseproof paper.

Mix together the oil, honey, cinnamon and salt in a large bowl. Add the oats and nuts, stirring well to combine.

Tip the mixture onto the baking tray and spread it out.

Bake for 20 minutes, stirring once halfway through. Don't panic if it still looks wet when it comes out. If you want clumps, press down on the granola before it cools, which will help it stick together.

Leave in the tray to cool completely before adding the dried fruit.

Pour it into a large sealed container where it will keep for up to 1 month.

GRANOLA & YOGHURT POPSICLES

These are an inventive way to get some goodness into fussy kids (and adults!). They are perfect for hot days, or when no one really wants to eat a heavy breakfast. You can even make them in ice lolly moulds to have on the way to school, nursery or work. You can flavour the yoghurt first if you want, too.

Makes 12

55g granola
(page 32)

150g yoghurt
(page 188)
50g frozen fruit

In a bowl, mix half the granola with half the yoghurt.

Divide the mixture into a 12-hole muffin tin or ice lolly moulds.

Add the frozen fruit on top of each one, then top with a spoonful of yoghurt.

Finally, sprinkle the remaining granola on top.

Freeze for at least 3 hours before tucking in.

BREAKFAST SUNDAE

This is a light breakfast that tastes more like a dessert so it's a win-win for kids. We know they're eating fruit, nice healthy yoghurt with no added sugar and getting some oats in their tummies to fill them up. They see something that looks like a fancy dessert and think they've won a watch!

Serves 4

3 tsp vanilla essence
400g yoghurt
(page 188)

150g frozen fruit (defrosted)
100g granola
(page 32)

Add the vanilla essence to the yoghurt and stir well to combine.

Spoon a layer of yoghurt into the bottom of 4 tall glasses or sundae dishes. Then alternate layers of fruit, granola and more yoghurt.

Serve immediately so the granola doesn't go soggy.

FLUFFY SCOTCH PANCAKES

Scottish pancakes are the ultimate weekend treat in my house. They can be topped with anything you want including chocolate spread, peanut butter, jam, bananas, frozen berries, honey and syrup . . . the possibilities are endless! Personally I like mine toasted with butter.

Serves 4

100g self-raising flour
¼ tsp baking powder
50g sugar
1 egg

60ml milk
Vegetable oil, to grease
Any toppings you like, to serve

Sieve the flour, baking powder and sugar into a bowl.

Add the egg and whisk together, gradually adding splashes of milk as you continue whisking. You want a relatively thick, smooth batter, about the same consistency as double cream.

Moisten a paper towel with vegetable oil, then use this to grease a thick-based frying pan. Put the pan on the hob over a medium-high heat and when it is hot, ladle in some of the batter.

As it starts to bubble on the surface, turn over the pancake and cook for 2 or 3 minutes until browned.

Enjoy with your favourite toppings! If you have leftovers, keep them in the fridge as a tasty snack for later. Just pop them in the toaster to reheat.

LOADED BREAKFAST BURRITOS

Bored of the usual breakfasts? These make a great hot breakfast with minimal fuss in the morning. They definitely taste like they cost a whole lot more than they do! I often make these at the weekend and then wrap and freeze for a quick and easy hot breakfast midweek.

Makes 12

Oil, for frying

2 sausages, removed from their skins

1 onion, diced

½ pepper, diced

1 tomato, diced

6 eggs

50ml milk

50g cheese, grated

Parsley, chopped

2 cooked potatoes or ½ tin, diced

12 wraps (page 197)

Pour a little oil into a frying pan and add the sausages, breaking them up with a wooden spoon (as you would if you were browning mince).

Add the diced onion and cook for 5 minutes.

Add the pepper and tomato and cook for a further 5 minutes.

Whisk the eggs in a bowl and add the milk.

Add this to the sausages and veg, and cook like you would scrambled eggs until the egg has cooked through.

Remove from the heat and add the grated cheese and parsley.

Stir through the potatoes.

Spoon the mixture onto 12 wraps and then either roll or fold them up, ready to eat.

If you're not eating them immediately, wrap each burrito in kitchen paper and freeze flat on a baking tray for at least an hour, before transferring them into freezer bags. You should be able to fit 4–6 in a bag depending on the size. Reheat in the microwave for 60–90 seconds.

SAUSAGE HASH

I created this dish whilst on holiday to use up some leftover ingredients, or fridge gravel, as I call it. I was amazed at how tasty it was – new favourite here!

Serves 4

1 tbsp oil, for frying

2 sausages, removed from their skins

1 onion, diced

2 tomatoes, diced

4 cooked potatoes or 1 tin, diced

1 tsp garlic powder

50g cheese, grated

Chopped parsley, to serve (optional)

Heat the oil in an oven-safe frying pan (or have an oven-safe dish ready for when you need to grill).

Fry the sausages, breaking them up with a wooden spoon (as you would if you were browning mince) until cooked.

Add the onion and cook for 2 minutes.

Add the tomatoes and cook for another 2 minutes.

Add the potatoes and the garlic powder and stir well. Cook for 5 minutes stirring occasionally.

Sprinkle the cheese on top and then place the pan under a hot grill until browned and the cheese has melted. Remove from the grill and scatter over the parsley if using.

JAMMY HEART FRENCH TOAST

This has become a bit of a treat in our house. Birthdays, Christmas, Easter, celebrating a particular achievement or sometimes just because Mum is in a good mood!

Serves 4

Knob of butter,
for frying
4 eggs
250ml single cream

1 tsp icing sugar, plus extra to
decorate
1 tsp vanilla essence
8 slices of bread
Jam (page 190)

Grease a large frying pan with butter and heat over medium heat.

Add all the ingredients, except the bread and jam, to a large bowl and whisk thoroughly.

Dip the bread into the mixture, and transfer to the frying pan 2 at a time, cooking for 2 minutes on each side.

Cut a love heart out of one piece of bread. Spread jam on the other slice and then sandwich them together.

Fill the heart hole with a little more jam and sprinkle some icing sugar over before serving.

ITALIAN BAKED EGGS

I made these for the first time recently after stumbling upon a similar recipe online. As usual, I adapted it to fit our budget and tested it out on my family. There were clean plates all round and everyone was happy!

Serves 4

Oil, for cooking

2 sausages, removed from their skins

1 onion, diced

400g tomato base sauce (page 167) or 1 x 400g tin chopped tomatoes

2 tsp garlic powder

2 tsp oregano (or Italian mixed herbs)

4 eggs

Part-baked baguette, sliced

50g cheese, grated

Preheat the oven to 180°C/Fan 155°C/Gas 4.

Heat the oil in a pan and fry the sausages, breaking them up with a wooden spoon (as you would if you were browning mince) until cooked.

Add the onion and cook for a couple of minutes until translucent.

Add the tomato sauce, garlic and oregano (or mixed herbs, if using) and stir well. Reduce the heat and simmer for 2 minutes.

Tip the mix into a casserole dish or split into 4 ramekins.

Crack the eggs on top and then place in the oven for 12–15 minutes.

While that's cooking, make the cheesy toast. Under the grill, toast the bread on one side. Cover the other side with cheese and return to the grill until bubbling.

Serve the baked eggs with the cheesy toast, and tuck in.

CHEESY QUESADILLAS

Another quick, easy, tasty breakfast (or lunch or snack) that can use up all those little bits of fridge gravel. Most combos work really well!

> **Makes 4**

8 wraps
(page 197)

100g cheese, grated
Any cooked meat or
veg you fancy

Heat a dry frying pan over medium heat and add one wrap.

Scatter over a little of the grated cheese along with any other filling you're using. Top with more grated cheese and the second wrap, to make a sandwich.

Cook for 2–3 minutes and then flip over with a large fish slice or spatula. Cook for another 2–3 minutes.

Repeat the process with the remaining wraps and filling, then slice into quarters and serve.

EGG MACMUFFINS

I'll let you decide where the inspiration for these came from, LOL! This is a great recipe to batch cook – just increase the ingredients, and you'll have breakfast muffin backups, which you can freeze!

Makes 12

Oil, for cooking
4 sausages
4 eggs
50ml milk

4 English muffins
4 slices of cheese

Tomato sauce, to serve

Squeeze out the sausage meat from the skin and shape into 4 patties.

Heat a frying pan over medium heat. Add the sausage patties and cook until they are brown.

Once cooked, remove from the pan and wipe it clean with kitchen paper. Return the pan to the hob and heat.

In a bowl, mix the eggs with the milk, and pour into the frying pan, cooking to make a very thin omelette.

Using a cookie cutter a similar size to your muffins, cut out circles from the omelette.

Slice the muffins in half and lightly grill them. You can also put the patties under the grill to keep them warm.

Sit a slice of cheese on top of each patty and allow to melt.

Assemble the muffins and top with a dollop of tomato sauce before serving.

To freeze, assemble the muffins, let them cool completely and wrap tightly before freezing. To reheat pop them in the microwave for a couple of minutes.

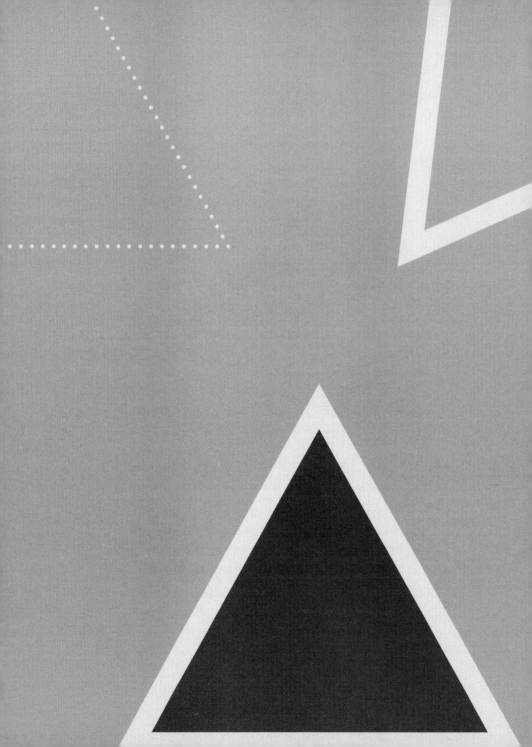

SOUPS & SALADS

POTATO & LEEK SOUP

Perfect for a busy weeknight, this is one of the cheapest recipes in the book with the added bonus of being both filling and tasty. As with most of my soups, this one's good for freezing in individual portions and eating later in the month.

 Serves 4 + 4 Leftover Portions

2 knobs of butter

300g frozen leeks, chopped

3 medium potatoes,
peeled and diced

2 garlic cloves, crushed

Salt and pepper

1l vegetable stock

Dash of milk

1 tbsp parsley, chopped

Part-baked baguette,
to serve

Melt the butter in a pan over a medium heat.

Add the leeks and fry until they just begin to colour, then add the potatoes and garlic and continue to fry so the potatoes get basted in the butter.

Add in salt and pepper to season, then pour in the stock. Put a lid on top and cook until the potatoes are soft, about 10 minutes.

Blitz the soup with a hand blender (or potato masher) then add in the milk and parsley.

Serve with part-baked baguette.

SCOTCH BROTH

I was brought up on this as it's my nana's weekly staple. She would make a pot on a Saturday and we would all go to hers after church on Sunday to have soup and toasties. If you're following the meal plan, you'll make three batches of this and you'll want to use the stock and some leftover meat from your roast gammon (page 87). If you haven't made it, you can make the stock using a ham hock, as below

 Serves 4 + 4 Leftover Portions

200g broth/soup mix
Ham hock
3l cold water
2 ham stock cubes
4 carrots, grated
2 onions, grated

50g frozen leek
2 potatoes,
peeled and cut into chunks

Part-baked baguette,
to serve

Soak your broth or soup mix overnight in plenty of cold water.

If you're making the ham stock from scratch, put the ham hock into a large pot and cover with the cold water. Bring to the boil and simmer for 1 hour. Remove the ham from the water and set it aside, saving the water, which is now a stock.

Add the drained and rinsed broth or soup mix and stock cubes to the stock, bring to the boil and simmer for an hour. Then add the veg and cook for another hour.

Cut the fat from your cooled ham and strip away all the meat (trying not to eat most of it – it's so delicious!).

Put a third of it back into the soup and freeze the rest for later.

Serve with part-baked baguette.

TOMATO SOUP

You just can't get simpler than this – everyone should know how to make tomato soup. If you've got kids this is perfect as it has none of the salt and sugar found in tinned soup. That's the best thing about home cooking – you can control the amount of salt and sugar your kids eat. I give methods below for cooking this soup either in a pan or in a slow cooker.

 Serves 4 + 4 Leftover Portions

2 onions diced

6 carrots sliced

2 tsps garlic powder

500ml vegetable stock

400g tomato base sauce
(page 167)

1 tsp parsley

1 tsp coriander

50g red lentils

Salt and pepper,
to taste

Part-baked baguette,
to serve

Add all your ingredients to a large saucepan or slow cooker.

If cooking in a pan:
Bring to the boil.

Reduce heat and simmer for 30 minutes.

If using a slow cooker:
Cook on high for 4–6 hours or low for 8–10 hours.

Once your soup is cooked blitz with a hand blender and season with salt and pepper to taste.

Serve with part-baked baguette.

CHICKEN & RICE SOUP

Not only is this soup tasty, filling and healthy, it's also super-easy to make.
If you're following the 8 week plan, the main ingredient is the roast chicken
(page 88) you had on Sunday. If you don't have any leftover chicken though, just
add a raw chicken breast when you put the stock in. Increase the simmer time
to 30 minutes and then remove the chicken and shred it using two forks before
adding back in.

 Serves 4 + 4 Leftover Portions

4 tbsp butter
1 onion, finely diced
50g frozen pepper, chopped
2 tbsp flour
150ml milk
1l chicken stock
1l water

50g frozen sweetcorn
180g uncooked rice
50g chicken, shredded
Seasoning, to taste

Part-baked baguette,
to serve

Melt 2 tablespoons of butter in a large saucepan and fry the onion
and peppers for 5 minutes over a medium heat, then tip them onto
a plate when done.

Melt the remaining butter in the same pan and use the flour to make a
roux by stirring it in with a whisk, then adding the milk and whisking
until it is a very thick but smooth sauce.

Whisk in the stock and the water.

Add the sautéed veg, sweetcorn and rice and simmer for 15 minutes
before adding the chicken.

Season to taste and serve with part-baked baguette.

PEA & HAM SOUP

This is a classic soup that is extremely filling and tasty! A true winter warmer.
Ham stock packs in so much flavour.

 Serves 4 + 4 Leftover Portions

1 knob of butter

1 onion, finely diced

1 medium potato, peeled and diced

1l ham stock

500g frozen peas

100g cooked ham with fat removed (use leftover gammon if you have it), chopped

Seasoning, to taste

Part-baked baguette, to serve

Melt the butter in a large saucepan over a medium heat and add in the onions. Cook until they've softened but without them starting to colour.

Add in the diced potato and toss in the onions.

Pour over the stock and simmer for about 10 minutes until the potato has softened.

Tip in the peas and bring back to the boil to cook for about 2 minutes.

Remove from the heat and blitz with a hand blender. Check the seasoning and add some more if needed.

Stir through the ham, allowing it to warm.

Serve with part-baked baguette.

MINESTRONE

My son loves this soup. I'm not 100 per cent sure if it's because it's so tasty or because I put the spaghetti in a freezer bag and let him bash it up!

 Serves 4 + 4 Leftover Portions

1 tbsp cooking oil

1 large onion, diced

4 carrots, diced

2 garlic cloves, thinly sliced

400g tomato base sauce (page 167) or 1 x 400g tin chopped tomatoes

1 x 400g tin baked beans

2 bay leaves

2 tsp dried basil

2 tbsp tomato purée

1.5l vegetable stock

100g frozen spinach

100g spaghetti, broken up

Salt and pepper, to taste

Part-baked baguette, to serve

Heat the oil in a large pan over a medium heat.

Add the onions and carrots and cook for a few minutes.

Add the garlic and cook for 2 minutes more.

Now add the tomato purée and cook for another minute.

Add in all the other ingredients and stir. Simmer for 15–20 minutes.

Serve with part-baked baguette.

PARSNIP SOUP

Parsnips are an underrated but cheap veg with a strong flavour that adds a kick to soup. This can be left chunky or blitzed for a smooth soup.

 Serves 4 + 4 Leftover Portions

4 tbsp butter
1 onion, chopped
1 tsp salt
1 clove garlic, crushed
1kg parsnips, peeled and chopped

1l chicken or vegetable stock
450ml milk
Seasoning, to taste

Part-baked baguette to serve

Melt the butter in a large pot over a medium heat.

Add the onion and salt. Cook, stirring occasionally until the onion is a bit translucent looking, about 10 minutes. Adjust the heat, if needed, so the onions cook but don't start to brown.

Add the garlic and cook, while you stir, for about 1 minute.

Add the parsnips and the stock and bring to the boil. Reduce the heat to a simmer and cook for about 20 minutes, then remove from the heat.

If you want a smooth soup, purée using a hand blender (or if you don't have one use a potato masher).

Add the milk and gently heat, stirring occasionally, until nice and hot all the way through. Don't let it boil! If it's too thick, add a bit more milk to loosen it.

Season to taste and serve with part-baked baguette.

FRENCH ONION SOUP

I'm not sure why this isn't as popular as other soups, it's just as easy and tasty –
and it looks really fancy, but is actually quite simple.

 Serves 4 + 4 Leftover Portions

1 part-baked baguette	2 tbsp plain flour
50g butter	1.5l strong beef stock
1 tbsp cooking oil	4 tsp garlic powder
1kg onions, finely sliced	1 tbsp Worcester sauce
1 tsp sugar	50g cheese, grated

Cook the part-baked baguette in the oven as per the instructions.
Once cooked leave to cool.

Heat the butter and oil in a large pan over a medium heat. Add the
onions and fry for 10 minutes.

Add the sugar, reduce the heat and cook for 20 minutes until the
onions are caramelised.

Add the flour and stir through.

Add the stock, garlic powder and Worcester Sauce and simmer for
20 minutes.

Slice the baguette and grill one side. Sprinkle the other side with
grated cheese and grill.

Pour the soup into bowls and then drop in a quarter of the cheese-
toasted baguette.

Serve with the remaining bread on the side.

CHICKEN NOODLE SOUP

This is the ultimate comfort food, made in an extra large batch that will keep you fed for three meals!

 Serves 4 + 4 Leftover Portions

1 knob of butter
2 tbsp cooking oil
3 onions, sliced
3 carrots, peeled and sliced
3 tsp garlic powder
2 chicken breasts,
cooked and shredded

2l chicken stock
1 tbsp parsley, chopped
2 nests of noodles
Seasoning, to taste
Dash of soy sauce (optional)

Heat the butter and oil in a large pot over a medium heat. Add in the onions and carrots and fry them for about 5 minutes without letting them brown.

Add in the garlic, chicken, stock and half of the parsley.

Bring to the boil and add the noodles.

Reduce to a simmer and cook the noodles as per the instructions on the packet, then season with salt and pepper.

Serve with a dash of soy sauce if desired and more parsley to taste.

Freeze the remainder in individual portions for lunch later in the month.

LENTIL SOUP

This recipe makes for a simple, cheap weeknight dinner. It's also the perfect way to sneak in some veg, which is then blended, hiding the evidence from fussy kids.

 Serves 4 + 4 Leftover Portions

1 tbsp cooking oil
6 medium carrots, diced
2 small onions, diced
3l ham or vegetable stock

300g red lentils

Part-baked baguette,
to serve

Heat the oil in a large saucepan.

Fry the carrots and onions for a couple of minutes until they've softened a little.

Add the stock and lentils. Bring to the boil and then reduce the heat. Simmer for 20 minutes stirring occasionally.

Blitz with a hand blender to desired consistency.

Serve with part-baked baguette.

TOMATO & LENTIL SOUP

This is a twist on my lentil soup (page 55) with some red chilli flakes to give it a bit of a kick. Just reduce the chilli if you have kids who are less keen on it.

 Serves 4 + 4 Leftover Portions

1 tbsp cooking oil
6 medium carrots, diced
2 small onions, diced
2 tbsp chilli flakes
3l vegetable or ham stock

2 x 400g tinned tomatoes
300g red lentils

Part-baked baguette,
to serve

Heat the oil in a large saucepan over a medium heat. Fry your diced carrots and onions for a couple of minutes until they've softened a little.

Add the chilli flakes and stir for 1 minute.

Then add your stock, tomatoes and lentils.

Bring to the boil, then reduce the heat and simmer for 20 minutes, stirring occasionally.

Blitz with a hand blender to your desired consistency.

Serve with part-baked baguette.

ONE-POT NOODLES

This is a dish based on a popular convenience food but with none of the nasties! It can be made at home in a pot or put in a flask or container to be made up later in the day with hot water. I usually make this with peas and sweetcorn, but you can use any thinly sliced leftover veg you might have in the fridge. If you're following the 8 week plan, you'll have leftover meat from your roast chicken (page 88).

Serves 2

50g leftover cooked chicken, shredded

1 nest of noodles

2 carrots, grated

Handful of frozen peas

Handful of frozen sweetcorn

1 chicken stock cube, halved

500ml boiling water

Divide up the chicken, noodles, veg and stock cube into two pots, plastic containers or flasks.

When ready to eat, pour 250ml of boiling water into each container and leave for 3–5 minutes covered loosely.

This one's fab for a take-to-work lunch. Just add boiling water whenever you're ready to eat it!

CHICKPEA & SPINACH SALAD

A quick, easy, cheap and tasty salad that is super-healthy and full of protein. The chickpeas make it way more filling than your average salad and the peppers add some lovely colour to your plate.

Serves 12

1 x 400g tin chickpeas
200g spinach
1 red pepper, sliced
1 orange or yellow pepper, sliced
6 spring onions, sliced

DRESSING
75ml olive oil
50ml lemon juice
¼ tsp salt
⅛ tsp black pepper

In a large bowl, combine the chickpeas, spinach, peppers and spring onions.

To make the dressing, in another bowl thoroughly combine the oil, lemon juice, salt and pepper.

When ready to serve, pour the dressing over the salad and give it a good mix.

SIMPLE MINT SALAD

This salad goes so well with the spicy salmon fishcakes (page 94). It's easy and cheap, specially as I use home-grown mint that I can pick fresh as needed.

Serves 4

½ head of lettuce, roughly torn up
2 carrots, grated

½ cucumber, sliced
2 tbsp mint
2 tbsp plain yoghurt

In a large bowl, add the lettuce, carrots, cucumber and mint.

Mix the yoghurt through the salad and serve immediately.

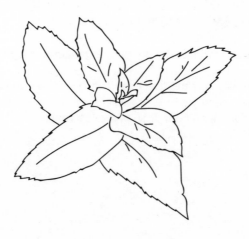

59
Soup & Salads

COOL BEAN SALAD

I had something similar to this in a restaurant with flatbreads and spicy chicken. It was amazing so I tried to replicate it at home. I'm pretty pleased with the results!

Serves 4

150g cooked long grain rice
2 x 400g tins mixed beans
50g sweetcorn
6 spring onions, diced

DRESSING
1 orange pepper, diced
2 tbsp coriander
½ tsp garlic powder

½ tsp salt
1 tsp cumin
¼ tsp black pepper
1 tsp smoked paprika
1 tbsp sugar
2 tbsp olive oil
2 tsp lime juice
2 tbsp white wine vinegar

In a large bowl, combine the first four ingredients.

In another bowl, combine the dressing ingredients and mix.

Pour the dressing over the rice, beans and veg and stir well to coat.

Put in the fridge for an hour or so before serving.

SIMPLE CARROT SALAD

As simple as the name suggests, and an easy way to get some veg into the diet – I also like to use my home-grown chives and parsley. This tastes especially good when served with my tuna fishcakes (page 94).

Serves 4

4 large carrots, grated
2 tbsp chives
2 tbsp parsley, chopped
½ x 400g tin chickpeas
2 tbsp olive oil

2 tbsp lemon juice
2 tsp honey
1 tsp mustard
½ tsp ground cumin
¼ tsp of fine sea salt

In a large bowl, combine the carrots, chives, parsley and chickpeas.

To make the dressing, add all the remaining ingredients to a small bowl and mix well.

Pour the dressing over the salad and serve immediately.

COUSCOUS & HARISSA VEG SALAD

I wasn't a fan of couscous before I came up with this recipe.
Now I love it! You can sub in/out whatever veg you like. Sweet potato is nice
as are those packets of Mediterranean veg you can often find reduced in the
supermarket! Just make sure all your veg is chopped
into similar-sized chunks.

Serves 4

2 tbsp olive oil
1 tbsp harissa paste
1 red pepper, chopped
1 yellow pepper, chopped
1 courgette, chopped
1 red onion, chopped
½ butternut squash, chopped

200g baby tomatoes
300ml vegetable stock
250g coucous
2 tbsp garlic powder
2 tbsp lemon juice
2 tsp parsley

Preheat the oven to 200°C/Fan 180°C/Gas 6.

In a small bowl, mix the olive oil and harissa paste.

Put the veg (except for the tomatoes) on a baking tray and pour the
oil and harissa mix over them. Toss around to make sure everything
is evenly coated and roast in the oven for 30 minutes.

Remove from the oven and add the tomatoes. Toss again then put
the tray back in the oven for another 10 minutes.

Meanwhile, heat the vegetable stock.

Put the couscous in a large bowl and pour over the hot vegetable stock and the garlic powder.

Cover and leave to absorb for 15 minutes.

Give the couscous a stir and then add the roasted veg.

Pour the lemon juice over and sprinkle the parsley on top.

This is
delicious hot or cold!

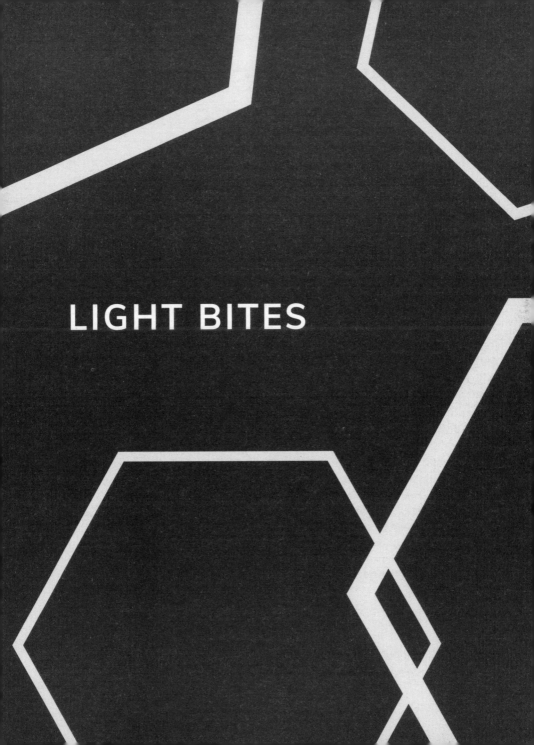

LIGHT BITES

MINI CRUSTLESS QUICHES

This recipe is so adaptable and a great way to use up fridge gravel! Add any veg and cooked meat you like. They're great for packed lunches. I usually serve up 2 for the adults and 1 for a child. You can freeze them too, just wrap them tightly then defrost in the fridge overnight.

Makes 8

Butter and flour, for greasing
(unless using a non-stick
muffin tray)
2 slices of bacon, diced
1 onion, diced

3 eggs
Splash of milk
150g cheese, grated
1 tomato, chopped

Preheat the oven to 200°C/Fan 180°C/Gas 6.

If you own the genius that is a silicone muffin tray (my favourite kitchen item) this is a good time to use it. If you don't, simply grease a regular muffin tray with butter and add a little plain flour to each hole, shaking around so each hole is totally coated in flour. Shake out the excess flour and discard. Now your muffin tray is non-stick!

In a pan over a medium heat, fry the bacon and onion together until the bacon is cooked.

In a bowl, whisk the eggs and milk, then add the cheese and tomato to the egg mix.

Add in the bacon and onion, then pour the mix into the muffin tray.

Bake for about 15 minutes until they start to go golden brown. They need to be cooked through, especially if you're planning to freeze for later.

PIZZA PIN WHEELS

This is a huge family favourite, which are great for picnics, buffets and lunch boxes as a variation on sandwiches. On special occasions, I switch out the savoury ingredients for sweet ones. Chocolate spread and mini marshmallows work a treat, just don't overload it or it will get MESSY!

Makes 8	

1 x 320g packet puff pastry
2 tbsp tomato base sauce (page 167)

Leftover cooked ham and veg
50g cheese, grated
Black pepper, to season

Preheat the oven to 200°C/Fan 180°C/Gas 6 and line a baking tray.

Roll out the puff pastry into a rectangle about 1cm thick.

Spread over the tomato sauce and add the ham, veg and cheese (or whichever other ingredients you've got in your fridge) and season with black pepper.

Roll up lengthways into a large sausage shape, and slice into 8 pieces.

Lay out the pin wheels on the baking tray.

Cook for 10–15 minutes until the pastry is a golden colour and the cheese is melted and bubbly.

BACON & CHEESE TURNOVERS

If you're a follower of FYF you'll know that this recipe was what launched us! People talk about 'going viral'. Well, this was our going viral moment! I always use mozzarella but any cheese works.

Makes 8

1 x 320g packet of puff pastry
8 slices bacon

100g cheese, grated

Preheat the oven to 180°C/Fan 160°C/Gas 4 and line or grease a baking tray.

Roll out the pastry to about 1cm thick. Cut into 8 squares.

Place the bacon diagonally on top of each square then add

the cheese on top of the bacon.

Fold over 2 corners of the pastry to meet in the middle and crimp the edges together.

Bake for 15 minutes, until the pastry is golden brown, the bacon is cooked and the cheese bubbling.

> Add some chilli jam or relish,
> or marmite underneath the bacon

CHEESE PUFFS

These are a massive favourite with anyone who has ever tried them! They're great as a light lunch or a side, and go really well with the tomato base sauce (page 167) for dipping.

Serves 4

1 egg
125ml milk
150g self-raising flour

200g strong Cheddar, grated
1 tsp mustard powder or cayenne pepper (optional)

Preheat the oven to 180°C/Fan 160°C/Gas 4 and line a baking tray.

In a large bowl, beat together the egg and milk,

Add the flour, cheese and mustard powder or cayenne pepper, if using.

Drop tablespoon-sized dollops onto the baking tray and bake for about 20 minutes.

Cool on a wire rack, then enjoy. If you like, you can serve with tomato base sauce.

ARANCINI

This is a great way to use up any rice dish leftovers. It's always a winner in my house and looks much fancier than it is. I've used jambalaya, but you can really use anything.

Makes 8

Leftover cold rice dish

100g cheese, cut into small chunks

100g plain flour

2 eggs, beaten

200g breadcrumbs

Vegetable oil, for frying

Salt, to season

Prepare two baking trays – line one with kitchen paper (you'll use this one for the arancini after being fried).

With damp hands, divide the rice mix into golfball-sized balls and flatten each piece into a disc. Then place a chunk of cheese in the middle and shape the disc around the cheese to form a ball.

Put the flour, eggs and breadcrumbs into three separate bowls then coat the balls first in flour, then in egg and finally in the breadcrumbs. Place them on the unlined baking tray.

Fill a deep pan with enough oil to cover the balls completely and set over a high heat. Test if it's hot enough by dropping in breadcrumbs. If they sizzle, it's ready.

MINI HOTPIES

This is great for using the leftover fillings from bigger pies. I make them in a muffin tray using homemade pastry. You only use a tiny amount of filling but because of the shortcrust pastry, the pies feel substantial. I always make two kinds in one go, because everyone has a favourite, but if you like, you can make them all with mince or all chicken. I always use the leftovers from the hearty beef pie to make the mini beef pies and leftovers from the chicken and sweetcorn pie to make the chicken pies.

Serves 2

2 portions shortcrust pastry (page 196)

Leftover mince from the hearty beef pie (page 80)

Leftover chicken filling from the chicken and sweetcorn pie (page 84), or you can use leftover veg, gravy and chicken from the Sunday roast chicken (page 88)

Preheat the oven to 200°C/Fan 180°C/Gas 6 and grease a 12-hole muffin tray.

Remove the pastry from the fridge and split it into 2 balls.

Roll out one and cut circles large enough to fit in the muffin tray.

Fill each pastry case with a little leftover meat, veg or gravy, depending on your filling choice.

Roll out the rest of the pastry and cut smaller circles to top your pies, pricking a hole in the top to let steam out.

Repeat the steps above until all the pies are assembled.

Bake for 20–25 minutes or until golden brown.

A serving is 2 pies for adults, 1 for kids!

FRITATTA

Quick, tasty and easy to make when you're short of time!

1 tbsp cooking oil
3 bacon rashers, chopped
1 onion, finely diced
100g frozen spinach

6 eggs
Salt and pepper, to season
100ml milk
40g Cheddar cheese, grated

Preheat the oven to 180°C/Fan 160°C/Gas 4 and line a small loaf tin with greaseproof paper.

Heat the oil in a pan over a medium heat. When hot add the bacon and fry for 2 minutes.

Add the onions and cook for another 4 minutes. Add the spinach and let it wilt for 2 minutes.

Meanwhile, crack the eggs into a bowl and season with salt and pepper. Whisk well and add the milk until combined. Add in half the cheese.

Pour the bacon mix out onto a piece of kitchen paper and allow to drain and cool slightly.

Add the bacon mix and eggs to the loaf tin, and top with the remaining cheese.

Bake for 20–25 minutes until golden and set.

CHEESY LENTIL BAKE

This is a fairly old-fashioned recipe that is extremely cheap to make but you wouldn't know that when you're eating it! It may be an unusual combination and not something you would often see in a recipe book but it's delicious. Tasty, filling and meat-free.

Serves 4

1 tbsp cooking oil
1 onion, chopped
1 carrot, chopped
1 celery stick, chopped
150g red lentils
1 garlic clove, crushed
420ml vegetable stock

100g cheese, grated
2 tbsp parsley
1 egg, beaten
Salt and pepper, to season
2 tomatoes, sliced
2 tbsp breadcrumbs

Preheat the oven to 180°C/Fan 160°C/Gas 4.

Heat the oil in a large saucepan over a medium heat. Add the onion and fry for a few minutes until soft.

Add the carrot, celery, lentils, garlic and stock and put a lid on the pan. Bring it to the boil then simmer for about 20 minutes or until all the stock is absorbed.

Add 75g of the cheese, the parsley and the egg to the lentil mixture and stir thoroughly. Season well.

Spoon into a shallow ovenproof dish and smooth the top. Top with the tomatoes. Mix the breadcrumbs with the remaining cheese and sprinkle over the dish.

Bake until the topping is golden brown and crisp, about 30 minutes, but keep checking so it doesn't burn.

COLCANNON

A traditional regional old-school recipe, which gives you the perfect opportunity to use up leftovers. The add-on of a poached egg lifts this to another level.

Serves 4

400g potatoes, unpeeled and diced
200g frozen swede
1 tbsp oil
1 onion, finely sliced

200g frozen cabbage
1 egg yolk
40g cheese, grated
Salt and pepper, to season
Poached eggs, to serve

Preheat the oven to 200°C/Fan 180°C/Gas 6.

Add the potato and swede to a large saucepan of water. Bring to a boil then simmer until they are soft, about 15 minutes.

Meanwhile, heat the oil in a large pan over a low heat and fry the onion and cabbage for about 5 minutes until softened.

Drain the potato and swede and roughly mash them before adding the cabbage and onion.

Stir in the egg yolk and season with salt and pepper.

Transfer the mixture to an ovenproof dish and sprinkle over all of the cheese.

Bake for 20 minutes, then serve with poached eggs.

MEAT
&
FISH

STEAK & SAUSAGE PIE

This is a Scottish staple often eaten at Hogmanay, but thank goodness it is not limited to one occasion! You can prepare the pie filling in the slow cooker or in the oven.

Serves 4

Salt and pepper, to season
1 tbsp flour
250g stewing beef steak
6 sausages, cut into chunks
1 tbsp cooking oil
2 onions, sliced
4 garlic cloves, chopped
850ml beef stock

2 bay leaves
Dash of Worcester sauce
1 tbsp parsley, chopped
Cornflour paste (1 tbsp cornflour mixed with 2 tbsp cold water)
1 x 340g packet puff pastry
1 egg, beaten, to glaze

Add some salt and pepper to the flour, then use the seasoned flour to dust the beef and sausage.

Heat the oil in a large pan and add the meat. Brown on all sides before removing with a slotted spoon. Place the meat to drain on kitchen paper.

Add the onions to the same pan and coat in the oil, cooking until they soften.

Add the garlic, then add a little stock and scrape the pan of the floury meaty bits, which will thicken out the liquid.

Add the meat back into the pan as well as the remaining stock, bay leaves and Worcester sauce. Season with salt and pepper.

Pour the mixture into the slow cooker, cooking on low for 8–10 hours or cook in the oven for 4 hours at 170°C/Fan 150°C/Gas 3.

Once cooked, stir through the parsley, and thicken the meat juices with the cornflour paste before pouring the mixture into a pie dish.

Heat the oven to 200°C/Fan 180°C/Gas 6 and roll out the pastry so it's large enough to lay over the steak and sausage mix. Brush the pastry with the beaten egg then bake for 20 minutes or until the pastry is golden brown.

Serve with boiled potatoes and root mash (page 178).

HEARTY BEEF PIE

When people look at this dish for the first time, they never believe it will feed a family of four. The beauty of this pie is all in the disguise – not only do we bulk out the mince with porridge oats (I know, it sounds odd, but trust me, no one will know and the meat stretches much further), but by using your staple homemade pastry, you're really making the most of what you have. This recipe makes enough mince for two other recipes: mini hotpies (page 71) and cottage pie (page 82). I advise making the mini hotpies at the same time as this and freezing them, if you have time. For the cottage pie, freeze a third of this mince mixture until you're ready to use it.

Serves 4

1 tbsp cooking oil
400g beef mince
2 onions, diced
4 large carrots, grated
100g porridge oats

600ml beef stock
4 tbsp brown sauce
Shortcrust pastry
(page 196)

Add the oil to a large saucepan and set it over a medium heat.

Brown the mince and onion before adding in the carrots and porridge oats. Stir through.

Add in the beef stock and brown sauce and bring to the boil.

Reduce the heat and simmer for 20 minutes stirring every 5 minutes. If it starts to stick you can add a little water, but you want the mix to be thick and not too watery or your pie will have a soggy bottom!

Leave to cool before continuing onto the next step and assembling the pie.

Heat the oven to 200°C/Fan 180°C/Gas 6 and lightly grease a 23cm pie dish.

Split the pastry in half and roll out one half until it is big enough to line the pie dish.

Once the dish is lined, add the mince mix and spread out.

Roll out the rest of the pastry and top the pie, pinching the edges with a fork to form a seal.

Using a knife, make 2 incisions about 2.5cm wide at the top of the pie around the centre to let the steam out.

Bake for 20 minutes or until golden brown, then serve. I like to have it with buttery boiled potatoes and mixed veg.

COTTAGE PIE

If you're following the meal plan, this recipe will use your leftover mince mix from the hearty beef pie. This is a great way to save time by bulk-cooking and loving your leftovers! If you don't have leftovers, prepare the mince mix as on page 80, halving the amount of each ingredient used.

Serves 8

Leftover mince mix (page 80)

500g potatoes, peeled and chopped

Preheat the oven to 200°C/Fan 180°C/Gas 6.

In a large saucepan, add the potatoes and cover with cold water.

Bring to the boil for about 20 minutes, until a fork goes through them easily.

Drain the potatoes, then mash them thoroughly. You can use regular mashed potatoes with butter and milk, but it can make the pie go soupy.

Put the mince into a square casserole dish and top with the mash, scoring the top of the mash with a fork.

Cook in the oven for 30 minutes, then serve with mixed veg.

> Try adding some sweet potato to the mash topping and sprinkling some cheese on top.

CHICKEN HASH

If you're following the meal plan, you'll have leftover chicken from the Sunday roast chicken (page 88) which will give you a delicious mid-week twist on a breakfast favourite. Adding an egg is a stroke of genius!

Serves 8

500g potatoes, unpeeled and cut into small cubes
1 tbsp vegetable oil
1 onion, chopped
200g peppers, sliced
200g cooked chicken, diced

1 garlic clove, crushed
1–2 tsp paprika
½–1 tsp dried thyme
Salt and pepper, to season
Fried egg, to serve

In a large saucepan, add the potatoes and cover with cold water.

Bring to the boil for about 10 minutes, until just cooked and drain.

Heat the oil in a pan over a medium heat. Add the onion and fry until softened. This will take about 5 minutes.

Add in the peppers and fry for another 5 minutes.

Stir in the cooked potatoes and cook for another 5 minutes until they start to brown.

Add the chicken and garlic and stir, then sprinkle in the paprika, thyme, salt and pepper, and give it a good mix so it's all combined.

Serve hot with a fried egg (though it's really good on its own too).

> Add some grated cheese to the top before grilling.

CHICKEN & SWEETCORN PIE

This is my step-daughter's favourite dinner. She even says it's better than her high-end supermarket favourite! The leftovers for this can be used in the mini hotpies (page 71), so if you're following the meal plan, make sure to set aside a quarter of the mix. I make the mini hotpies at the same time as this and freeze them so they're ready when I need them.

Serves 4

200g leftover cooked chicken, cut into chunks
4 tbsp flour
1 tbsp cooking oil
30g butter

300ml chicken stock
100g sweetcorn
Shortcrust pastry (page 196)
1 egg, beaten, to glaze

Drench the chicken in 2 tbsp of the flour.

Heat the oil in a large saucepan and fry the chicken over medium heat until browned. Remove the chicken from the pan and set aside.

Melt the butter in the same pan and stir in the remaining 2 tbsp of flour. Cook for 2 minutes then stir in the chicken stock and whisk until smooth.

Add the chicken back in along with the sweetcorn. Simmer gently for 20 minutes.

Heat the oven to 200°C/Fan 180°C/Gas 6 and lightly grease a 23cm pie dish.

Split the pastry in half and roll out one half to line the pie dish. Then add the mix and spread out.

Roll out the rest of the pastry and top the pie, pinching the edges with a fork to form a seal. You can brush the beaten egg between the pie shell and top to help seal.

Make 2 cuts in the top of the pie around the centre to let the steam out. Brush the top of the pie with the beaten egg.

Bake for 20 minutes or until golden brown, then serve. I like to have it with boiled potatoes and mixed veg.

SPANISH CHICKEN

This delicious chicken dish, loaded with veg from the peppers and tomato sauce, is a twist on a classic Spanish chicken dish.

Serves 4

Cooking oil

2 chicken breasts, chopped into chunks

1 onion, chopped

2 garlic cloves, chopped

250ml chicken or vegetable stock

2 tbsp paprika

1 red pepper, chopped

1 green pepper, chopped

400g tomato base sauce (page 167) or 1 x 400g tin chopped tomatoes

2 tbsp tomato purée

Heat the oil in a saucepan over a medium heat and cook the chicken until golden, a couple of minutes.

Set the chicken aside, then in the same pan, add the onion and gently fry for a couple of minutes until soft, then add the garlic and fry for another minute.

Add the stock, paprika and chicken to the pan and bring to the boil. Add the peppers and reduce the heat to a simmer for about 10 minutes.

Add in the tomato base sauce and tomato purée, and leave to simmer gently for about 20 minutes.

Serve hot. This is great with mashed potatoes.

ROAST GAMMON

This is a cheap and fuss-free roast dinner with an added benefit of leaving you with stock which you can use in your scotch broth (page 47). You'll also get lots of leftover ham from this roast, which can be used in your pea & ham soup (page 50) or gammon picnic pasta (page 110).

Serves 4

1kg gammon joint
250ml water

2 tbsp honey

Add the gammon joint and water to a large saucepan and bring to the boil. Reduce the heat and simmer gently for 90 minutes.

Preheat the oven to 200°C/Fan 180°C/Gas 6.

Remove the joint from the water and place on a baking tray, making sure to save the water (which is now a ham stock!).

Pour the honey over the joint and rub all over.

Cook uncovered in the oven for 30 minutes, then leave to rest for 15 minutes once it's out, before carving.

Use half of the gammon in this meal and save the rest in 100g portions in freezer bags – it'll come in handy.

Serve with root mash (page 178) and roast potatoes (page 177).

ROAST CHICKEN

Everyone loves a roast chicken – it's cheaper than beef or lamb yet still tasty. You can also get another two meals out of this bird by stripping the chicken and using about 200g of the meat (breast, leg, anything you can get hold of) in your fakeaway chicken fried rice (page 132) and in the chicken & rice soup (page 49). Remember to use the carcass to make stock for your soup!

Serves 4

1 whole chicken
2 lemons, halved
½ onion
Butter or cooking oil
Salt and pepper,

to season
400g frozen vegetables (onion, celery and carrots all work well)
500ml white base sauce (page 168)

Preheat the oven to 200°C/Fan 180°C/Gas 6.

Remove the chicken from the fridge at least 20 minutes before starting to cook.

Put ½ a lemon and onion in the bottom end of the chicken and ½ a lemon in the other end.

Prick the chicken all over and squeeze another lemon half over the bird.

Rub the bird with butter or oil and grate over the zest of your squeezed lemon, then season with salt and pepper.

Add the vegetables to a roasting tray and sit the bird on top. Add the remaining lemon half to the tray.

Roast for 25 minutes per 500g, plus another 25 minutes on top of that.

Remove from the oven once roasted (the juices should run clear) and allow the bird to rest for 20 minutes. Squeeze any remaining juice from the roasted lemons over the chicken before carving.

Gently heat your white sauce and frozen veg together in a pan until warm. Serve with the roast chicken and fondant potatoes (page 174).

SAUSAGE MEATLOAF

My kids would eat this every day if I allowed them. It started off as a stuffing recipe made by my aunt and fought over at Christmas time as there was never enough. So I started serving it as a standalone dish and my kids still fight over it. If you miraculously have leftovers, slice it really thinly and eat cold. It tastes just like Haslet!

Serves 8

1 tbsp oil
2 onions, finely diced
6 sausages, removed from their skins

100g breadcrumbs
1 egg, beaten

Preheat the oven to 180°C/Fan 160°C/Gas 4 and line a small loaf tin with baking paper.

Heat the oil in a pan over a medium heat and fry the onions until soft. Tip onto a plate and let cool.

Add all the ingredients to a bowl and mix well.

Push the mixture into the tin and cover with foil.

Cook in the oven for 30 minutes, then remove the cover and cook for a further 15 minutes so the top browns.

Serve warm or cold. I like it with mashed potato, carrots and gravy.

CARAMELISED ONION & SAUSAGE STEW

An upscale version of sausage and mash, this is a good winter dish and a brilliant one-pot dinner for minimal washing up.

Serves 4

50g butter
1 onion, diced
1 tbsp demerara sugar
200g frozen carrots
200g frozen swede
1 garlic clove, crushed
1 tbsp tomato purée
450ml chicken or beef stock

400g tomato base sauce (page 167) or 1 x 400g tin chopped tomatoes
Splash of Worcester sauce
2 large potatoes, cut in chunks
8 cooked sausages, cut into chunks

Heat the butter in a pan over a low heat, then add the sliced onion and fry gently for 20 minutes, stirring occasionally to make sure they don't stick.

Add the sugar and increase the heat for 3 minutes.

Reduce the heat and add the carrots, swede, garlic and tomato purée and cook for 5 minutes.

Add the stock, tomato sauce or tinned tomatoes and Worcester sauce and simmer for another 5 minutes.

Add the potatoes and cook for 15 minutes or until soft.

Add the cooked sausages and stir through.

Serve hot. This goes nicely with mashed potato.

BACON, CHEESE & VEG HOTPOT

This started off as a very basic recipe which I adapted with my white base sauce and extra veg. Plates always come back clean after this dinner!

Serves 4

500g potatoes, thinly sliced
200g frozen cauliflower
200g frozen broccoli
200g frozen leeks
1 tbsp cooking oil

6 rashers of bacon, diced
2 onions, diced
500ml white base sauce (page 168)
200g cheese, grated

Preheat the oven to 200°C/Fan 180°C/Gas 6.

Bring a pan of water to the boil. Add the potato slices and the frozen veg and parboil for 5 minutes.

Drain well and allow to dry and cool down.

Add the oil to the pan and fry the bacon and onion lightly.

Layer the ingredients in a deep dish. Start with bacon and onion, spreading out half the mixture in the dish, then spread half the veg on top of that. Add a layer of potato slices and repeat.

Pour over your white sauce and then sprinkle the cheese on top.

Cook in the oven for 30 minutes and serve hot.

FISH PIE

A fish pie always seems like a bit of a luxury dish but by using cheaper white frozen fish it can be enjoyed often!

Serves 4

500g frozen white fish fillets
2 tbsp dried parsley
500ml white base sauce
(page 168)

200g frozen peas
500g cooked potato, mashed

Start by poaching the fish. Place the fish fillets in a saucepan and cover with boiling water fresh from the kettle.

Bring back to the boil and simmer for about 15 minutes.

When the fish is poached, lift it out with a slotted spoon onto a plate. Break up the fish with a fork into bite sized pieces.

Put the fish and the frozen peas into a 23cm pie dish.

Add the parsley to the white sauce and pour it over the peas and fish.

Top with mashed potato and score with a fork.

Place under a hot grill for about 5 minutes, until the mash has turned a lovely golden brown.

Add some grated cheese to the top before grilling.

TUNA FISHCAKES & SPICY SALMON FISHCAKES

Fishcakes are a great way to get those healthy omegas into your diet, so I've given two different recipes below. Cold mashed potato works best, but you can make it fresh too. These go well with a simple mint (page 59) or carrot salad (page 61).

Serves 4

TUNA FISHCAKES:
4 spring onions, sliced
1 garlic clove, crushed
20g butter
800g cooked potato, mashed
100g frozen sweetcorn, thawed
1 tsp parsley
2 x 110g tins of tuna, drained
Salt and pepper, to season

SALMON FISHCAKES:
4 spring onions, finely chopped
1 garlic clove, crushed
Cooking oil, for frying
500g cooked potato, mashed
1 tbsp chilli flakes
1 x 210g tin of salmon, drained
Zest of half a lemon
Salt and pepper, to season

PREP:
2 tbsp plain flour
1 egg, beaten
2 tbsp cold water
100g breadcrumbs
Cooking oil, for frying

Gently fry your spring onions and garlic in oil/butter for 2 minutes over a medium heat. Remove from the heat and place in a large bowl, leaving to cool slightly.

Once cool, add the rest of the fishcake ingredients. Mix well using your hands, then shape into patties.

Next, set up your 'fishcake prep line': three bowls, one with flour, the next with egg and cold water and the third with breadcrumbs.

Coat the fishcake in plain flour, then dip in the egg. Finally, coat in breadcrumbs. Repeat with the other fishcakes, then chill in the fridge until you're ready to cook.

Heat the oil in a large frying pan and shallow-fry the fishcakes for 4–5 minutes per side, until golden brown. Drain on kitchen paper.

Serve with simple mint or carrot salad.

FISH TRAYBAKE

Traybakes are quick, easy and adaptable – you vary what you add depending on different tastes and there's minimal washing up! But have you ever thought to make one with fish before? This fish traybake contains white fish and a bag of freezer veg which means it's one dish providing the whole family with healthy nutrients. Lots of people don't know what to do with fish outside of the usual take away. This is a great way to get fish into your diet without all the grease and oil of traditional fish and chips.

Serves 4

500g potatoes, cut into chunks
150g frozen broccoli
150g frozen sliced peppers
3 small onions, quartered
6 garlic cloves, unpeeled

1 lemon, quartered
450g frozen fish fillets
A good splash of cooking oil
Salt and pepper, to season

Preheat the oven to 180°C/Fan 160°C/Gas 4.

Bring a pan of water to the boil. Add the potatoes and parboil for 10 minutes.

Drain the potatoes and add them to a roasting tray along with the garlic and the rest of the veg.

Squeeze over the juice from 2 of the lemon quarters. Pour over the oil, season and toss well.

Put in the oven to roast, tossing every 10 minutes.

After 25 mins sit the fish on top of the veg and put back in the oven until it is cooked. This will take about 10–15 minutes depending on the size of the fillets.

Use the other lemon quarters to squeeze over the dish once cooked.

Add some freshly sliced fennel to
the traybake before cooking.

PASTA & RICE

5-A-DAY
SAUSAGE PASTA

This pasta dish uses your tomato base sauce, packed with hidden goodness (great for veg-refusers like my kids!). When making a pasta sauce my top tip is to add a ladle of the cooking water from the pan of cooked pasta to your sauce. The starch from the pasta is now in that water, so the sauce will cling to the pasta. It sounds strange, but it definitely works.

Serves 4 + 4 Leftover Portions

300g pasta
100g frozen spinach
100g frozen leek
100g frozen peas and sweetcorn
6 sausages

400g tomato base sauce (page 167) or 1 x 400g tin chopped tomatoes
1 tbsp paprika

Preheat the grill, ready to cook the sausages.

Bring a large saucepan of water to the boil and cook the pasta according to the packet instructions. Add the veg in 4 minutes before the end of the cooking time.

Grill the sausages until cooked through and allow to cool.

Heat your tomato base sauce or tinned tomatoes in a separate pan until piping hot, add the paprika, reduce heat and simmer.

Slice the sausages in half lengthways and then cut each piece into 4 chunks – it will stretch further and kids won't argue about who has more!

Once the pasta and veg are ready, take out 1 ladle of the cooking water and add it to the tomato sauce, stirring through.

Drain the pasta and veg and return them to the pan. Stir in the sausages and tomato sauce and mix thoroughly.

Serve straight away.

Add some sliced chorizo or grilled bacon pieces to the recipe to make it a bit special!

Remember to save half of this in the freezer for another day, just defrost in the fridge overnight before eating it!

CHEESY VEGGIE PASTA

This recipe introduces you to my legendary cheese sauce. Some people are wary of a white or cheese sauce as it takes time, but it's worth it as you can make a large vat of the white base sauce and keep it in individual portions in freezer bags. Trust me, once you've made this you won't ever go back to pricey jar or packet sauces. Remember to save half of this in the freezer for another day. Just defrost it in the fridge overnight before eating it!

  Serves 4 + 4 Leftover Portions

300g pasta	1l white base sauce
400g frozen mixed veg	(page 168)
	200g cheese, grated

Bring a large saucepan of water to the boil and cook the pasta according to the packet instructions.

Cook the veg in the same pan, a few minutes before the pasta is done.

Make your white base sauce or, if you're like me and keep reserves of it ready for any occasion, retrieve some from the freezer and heat it gently to defrost.

When the white sauce is ready stir in half the cheese and let it melt.

Once the pasta and veg are ready, take out 1 ladle of the cooking water and add it to the cheese sauce, stirring through.

Drain the pasta and veg and put into a large dish.

Pour over the cheese sauce and mix well.

Top with remaining cheese and put under the grill to melt for 5–10 minutes.

Add some cooked gammon or chicken for an extra flavour boost.

LASAGNE

If you've been following the 8 week plan, you'll have this ready in no time. Just use the bolognese leftovers and some white base sauce. If you're like me and keep a freezer bag of white sauce at the ready at all times, all you'll need is some pasta sheets and grated cheese. If you don't have bolognese leftovers, just make the bolognese fresh, halving the amount of each ingredient.

 Serves 6

Bolognese leftovers	500ml white base sauce
(page 125)	(page 168)
8 lasagne sheets	150g cheese, grated

Preheat the oven to 200°C/Fan 180°C/Gas 6.

Put a layer of bolognese into the base of a lasagne dish.

Lay half of the lasagne sheets on top.

Spoon over half of the white sauce.

Repeat with another layer of bolognese, lasagna sheets and white sauce.

Top with grated cheese.

Cook in the oven for 30 minutes then serve with sweetcorn or peas on the side.

> Add a tablespoon of Worcester sauce to the bolognese or, if you're feeling really luxurious, a couple of tablespoons of red wine!

EASY-PEASY PASTA

This is my kids' favourite pasta dish! It's so quick and easy, and leftovers will become a lunch for another day.

Serves 4 + 4 Leftover Portions

400g pasta
200g frozen cauliflower
200g frozen leeks
200g soft cheese

250ml vegetable stock
1 tsp garlic powder
1 tsp dried parsley
1 tsp dried basil

Bring a large saucepan of water to the boil and cook the pasta according to the packet instructions. Add the veg for the last 5 minutes of cooking.

To make the sauce, put the soft cheese and vegetable stock in another pan over a low-medium heat and stir until combined and smooth.

Add the garlic powder, parsley and basil.

Once the pasta and veg are ready, drain and return to the pan.

Stir in the sauce and then you're ready to serve.

Add some cooked diced bacon to this dish to make it even special.

Remember to save half of this in the freezer for another day. Just defrost it in the fridge overnight before eating it!

CREAMY
CAJUN CHICKEN PASTA

This is a twist for meat-lovers on my easy-peasy pasta for meat lovers. You can make it as spicy or mild as needed by adjusting how much Cajun spices you use. Leftovers will become a lunch another day!

 Serves 4 + 4 Leftover Portions

300g pasta
Cooking oil
250g chicken, diced
1 tbsp Cajun spices
600g frozen stir fry veg

200ml vegetable stock
200g cream cheese
Cornflour paste (1 tbsp cornflour mixed with 2 tbsp cold water)

Bring a large saucepan of water to the boil and cook the pasta according to the packet instructions.

Meanwhile, heat the oil in a wok then add the chicken. Sprinkle over half of the Cajun spices, and fry for 5 minutes.

Add the veg and sprinkle over the rest of the Cajun spices. Fry for 10 minutes.

To make the sauce, add the stock to a small saucepan and stir in the cream cheese until melted.

Once the pasta is ready, take out 2 ladles of the cooking water and add it to the sauce, stirring through.

Stir the cornflour paste into the sauce to thicken.

Drain the pasta, and add it, along with the sauce, to the chicken and veg and mix thoroughly. Serve hot!

Remember to save half of this in the freezer for another day. Just defrost it in the fridge overnight before eating it!

SAUSAGE PASTA BAKE

This is another way to use sausages and pasta which tastes completely different to my 5-a-day sausage pasta! I always get clean plates when I serve up this one!

 Serves 4 + 4 Leftover Portions

1 tbsp cooking oil

6 sausages, removed from their skins

2 garlic cloves, crushed

2 tsp dried basil

400g tomato base sauce (page 167) or 1 x 400g tin chopped

tomatoes

300g pasta

200g soft cheese

100g spinach

100g cheese, grated

100g cherry tomatoes, halved

Preheat the oven to 200°C/Fan 180°C/Gas 6.

Heat the oil in a frying pan over a medium heat and then stir in the sausage meat and cook as if you're browning mince, breaking it up using a wooden spoon.

When it's cooked, about 10 minutes, add the garlic and 1 teaspoon of the basil and cook for another 2 minutes.

Add the tomato base sauce or tinned tomatoes and bring to the boil, then reduce the heat and simmer for 10 minutes.

Meanwhile, bring a saucepan of water to the boil and cook the pasta until it's almost ready, for about 2 minutes less than the cooking time on the packet.

Remove the tomato sauce from the heat and stir in the soft cheese and spinach. Add a ladle of the pasta cooking water to the sauce.

Drain the pasta and put it into a shallow casserole dish, approximately 30 x 20cm, then pour over the sauce and stir well.

Top with grated cheese, cherry tomatoes and sprinkle the remaining basil on the top.

Bake in the oven for 10–15 minutes or until the cheese has melted and is golden brown.

Remember to save half of this in the freezer for another day. Just defrost it in the fridge overnight before eating it!

GAMMON PICNIC PASTA

A little unusual but perfect for picnics or buffets. If you're following the meal plan, this uses leftovers from your gammon Sunday roast (page 87). Just shred the gammon meat – it's way more substantial than it first looks. This recipe makes a double batch so love your leftovers and they will do you a nice lunch for another day.

 Serves 4 + 4 Leftover Portions

300g pasta
1 tbsp oil
5 tbsp mayonnaise
1 tsp mustard powder
1 tsp cayenne pepper

1 tbsp honey
6 spring onions, sliced
100g frozen sliced peppers, defrosted
100g cooked gammon shredded

Bring a large saucepan of water to the boil and cook the pasta according to the packet instructions.

Drain and rinse under cold water, then stir through the oil to stop it sticking together as it cools.

Add the mayonnaise, mustard powder, cayenne pepper and honey to a bowl and mix thoroughly.

Once the pasta is cold add all the sauce, veg and gammon and stir through ensuring it is all coated. Then serve cold.

Remember to save half of this in the freezer for another day, just defrost it in the fridge overnight before eating it!

TUNA PASTA BAKE

This one uses two of the recipes from the basics section: creamy white base sauce and tomato base sauce, meaning it's not only extra delicious, but also easy and cheap!

 Serves 4 + 4 Leftover Portions

300g pasta
100g sweetcorn
100g peas
250ml white base sauce (page 168)

250ml tomato base sauce (page 167), or ½ tin chopped tomatoes
200g cheese, grated
2 x 110g tins tuna, drained

Bring a large saucepan of water to the boil and cook the pasta according to the packet instructions. Cook the veg in the same pan, a few minutes before the pasta is done.

In another pan over a low-medium heat combine the white base sauce and tomato base sauce and whisk continually until they are well mixed.

Stir in half the cheese and let it melt into the sauces.

Before draining the pasta, add a ladle of the cooking water to the sauce and stir through.

Drain the pasta and veg and put them into a 30 x 20cm dish along with the tuna. Pour over the sauce and mix well.

Top with the remaining cheese and put under the grill to melt, about 10 minutes.

There will be enough of this left for lunch later in the month so cover your leftovers well and freeze.

GNOCCHI

These can be a little fiddly to make which is why most people buy them ready-made, but the effort is definitely worth it as they taste amazing, save you money (yay) and will impress most people! Don't throw away your potato skins either as you can use them to make potato peel crisps (page 179).

Serves 6

1kg potatoes
¾ tsp salt
1 egg yolk

130g plain flour, plus extra for dusting
400g tomato base sauce (optional, page 167)

Preheat the oven to 200°C/Fan 180°C/Gas 6.

Bake the potatoes for 1 hour or so, until soft on the inside. Alternatively, you can cook the potatoes in the slow cooker or use leftover baked potatoes.

After around 15–20 minutes when they're cool enough to handle, scoop out the potato flesh and mash until very smooth.

On a clean, dry surface, gather the potato into a mound, sprinkle with salt, then leave to cool completely, for around 15 minutes.

Put a large pan of water on to boil.

Pour the egg yolk onto the potato mound and then tip the flour on top.

Using a knife or metal spatula fold the flour and egg into the potato until combined. Don't overwork it or your gnocchi will be tough once cooked.

Gently squeeze and pat your mix until it resembles cookie or biscuit dough. It will be quite sticky, but if it's too sticky to work with, add more flour, one tablespoon at a time.

Divide your dough into quarters.

Working on a lightly floured surface with floury hands, roll each quarter into a long snake, about 2 cm wide.

With a sharp knife cut the snake into 2 cm pieces, then use your finger or a fork to gently press each piece slightly.

Adjust the heat so the water in your pan is simmering nicely and then cook your gnocchi in batches one snake's worth at a time.

When the gnocchi float to the top, they are ready – this should take only a couple of minutes – so remove them with a slotted spoon and place on a wire rack to cool.

You can now serve immediately with a tomato base sauce or, if you want to be adventurous, sautéed in a good knob of butter with some sliced garlic!

MEDITERRANEAN PASTA

Oily fish is really good for adults and growing kids alike, and this is a great way to get it into your diet if you're not a massive fan of fish. Defrost a portion of your tomato base sauce the night before to make this an easy meal.

Serves 4 + 4 Leftover Portions

400g spaghetti
2 tsp cooking oil
1 onion, chopped
1 garlic clove, crushed
1–2 pinches of chilli flakes
300g cherry tomatoes, halved
200g frozen peas

400g tomato base sauce (page 167) or 1 x 400g tin chopped tomatoes
120g tin of sardines in tomato sauce
1 tbsp dried basil
Black pepper, to season

Bring a large saucepan of salted water to the boil and cook the spaghetti according to the packet instructions.

Heat the oil in a pan. Add the onion and garlic and fry over a medium heat for 5–7 minutes until the onion has softened.

Stir in the chilli flakes, tomatoes, peas, tomato base sauce or tinned tomatoes and sardines with their sauce, roughly breaking up the sardines.

Cover and simmer for about 5 minutes or until the sauce is hot and the tomatoes have softened.

Stir in the basil and season with black pepper.

Once the pasta is ready, add 1 ladle of the spaghetti water to the sardine sauce.

Drain the spaghetti, and add to the sauce, tossing well to mix.

Remember to save half of this in the freezer for another day. Just defrost it in the fridge overnight before eating it!

CAJUN SPICY RICE

A bit like adding oats to mince, initially I wasn't sure this would work but now this recipe has become one of my faves. Perfect to throw together after a super-busy day when everyone is starving and asking when dinner is.

Serves 4

300g long grain rice
100g frozen peas
100g frozen sweetcorn
1 tbsp oil
2 onions, diced
200g minced beef

1 tbsp Cajun spices
2 tbsp Worcester sauce
150g frozen sliced peppers
200ml beef stock
4 spring onions, sliced

Cook the rice according to the packet instructions, adding the peas and sweetcorn to the same pan to cook.

In a large saucepan, heat the oil and add the onion and the mince. Cook over a medium heat until the mince has browned, breaking it up with a wooden spoon as you go.

Add the Cajun spices and Worcester sauce and stir through. Add the peppers and stir again.

Pour in the beef stock and simmer for 15–20 minutes.

Once the rice, peas and corn and cooked, stir them into the mince, adding the spring onions.

Give it a good stir and it's ready to serve.

EASY ONE-POT RICE

You can make this with pretty much ANY meat leftovers like chicken, gammon or sausage.

Serves 4

300g long grain rice
600ml vegetable stock
100g frozen sliced peppers
100g frozen sliced carrots
100g frozen peas

½ tsp turmeric
Salt and pepper, to taste
1 tbsp parsley
100g cooked meat leftovers

Put the rice into a saucepan and add the vegetable stock, vegetables and turmeric. Put the lid on and cook for about 15 minutes.

Add the salt and pepper, then continue to cook until all the stock has evaporated.

Stir the parsley and any cooked meat through and heat for 5 minutes, then it's ready to serve

HAWAIIAN FRIED RICE

This meal came about after we'd had gammon steaks and pineapple one night and had some leftovers to use up! At first, I wasn't sure on the combination of flavours but it works well! If you're using leftover cooked rice, remember the safety guidelines on reheating – make sure it's piping hot all the way through.

Serves 4

150g frozen cauliflower, defrosted
2 tbsp cooking oil
1 onion, diced
100g cooked gammon leftovers
300g rice, cooked and cooled

(day-old is best)
2 tbsp soy sauce
2 eggs
50g frozen pineapple chunks, defrosted

Blitz the cauliflower until it's a similar texture to rice. Use a food processor if you have one, but if not, you can grate the cauliflower instead.

Heat the oil in a wok or large frying pan over a medium heat and stir-fry the cauliflower 'rice' and onion together for 3 minutes.

Add the ham and cook for 2 minutes, continuing to stir.

Add in the actual rice and soy sauce, and stir until well combined.

Make a well in the centre of the wok and add the eggs, whisking until they start to resemble slightly undercooked scrambled egg.

Finally, add the pineapple, heat through for 2 minutes, and it's ready to serve!

SLOW COOKER

CHICKEN JAMBALAYA

This is John's favourite dinner. Tasty, healthy, cheap and when you do it as drop bag it saves masses of money. You can also do it on the stove if you're not in a rush. Your leftovers from this dish become arancini later in the month.

Serves 8

1 chicken breast, diced
1 onion, diced
150g frozen sliced peppers
2 garlic cloves, crushed
2 tbsp Cajun spice or smoked paprika
500g rice

400g tomato base sauce (page 167) or 1 x 400g tin chopped tomatoes
700ml chicken stock

Flatbread (page 197), to serve

Add all the ingredients except the chicken stock and flatbread to a large freezer bag and seal well.

Freeze until the night before you want to eat it and defrost overnight in the fridge.

'Drop' the bag's contents into the slow cooker and add the chicken stock.

Cook for 4–6 hours on high or 8–10 hours on low.

Serve with flatbread.

Add chorizo to this dish for a special treat!

KEEMA CURRY

This is basically a curried mince. Mince is great to bulk out and not an obvious choice when it comes to curry. That's where the money saving comes in. Sometimes it's good to step out of your comfort zone!

Serves 4

200g beef mince
100g red lentils
2 onions, finely chopped
2 tsp garlic powder
2 tbsp ground ginger
3 tbsp curry powder
100g diced potato

3 tbsp tomato puree
750ml vegetable stock
100g frozen peas
100g frozen carrots

Freshly boiled rice,
to serve

Add all the ingredients except the frozen peas and carrots, vegetable stock and rice to a large freezer bag and seal well.

Freeze until the night before you want to eat it and defrost overnight in the fridge.

'Drop' the bag's contents along with the vegetable stock into the slow cooker and cook for 4–6 hours on high or 8–10 hours on low. Add in the frozen peas and carrots for the last 10 minutes of cooking.

Serve with freshly boiled rice.

CHILLI CON CARNE

Another classic adapted into a drop bag, made special with the addition of a couple of squares of chocolate! I don't know how it affects the flavour but it seems to intensify it and make it smooth and creamy.

Serves 4

200g beef mince

100g lentils

2 onions, chopped

1 red pepper (or handful of frozen peppers), chopped

3 garlic cloves, chopped

1 x 400g tin kidney beans (or pinto, black or black-eyed if you have them)

400g tomato base sauce (page 167) or 1 x 400g tin chopped tomatoes

1 tsp chilli powder

2 tsp oregano

2 tsp cumin

285ml vegetable stock

2 squares dark chocolate, (optional)

Rice, to serve

Add everything, apart from the chocolate, vegetable stock and rice, to a large freezer bag and freeze.

Defrost in the fridge the night before you want it, then drop into the slow cooker.

Add the stock and cook for 4–6 hours on high or 8–10 hours on low.

Add the chocolate 1 hour before serving.

Serve with rice.

SPAGHETTI BOLOGNESE

This one's a classic family fave with a twist. The recipe here is for a double portion of bolognese, which you'll freeze and use later in the month. If you're following the 8 week plan you'll use your bolognese leftovers to make lasagne (page 104), but if you just want to make one batch, simply halve the ingredients! Here, I've bulked out the mince with red lentils. As with all drop bags, you can also cook this on the stove. Don't be concerned about refreezing once it is cooked as the rule of thumb is you can freeze once raw and once cooked.

Serves 4 + Leftovers

400g beef mince
200g red lentils
4 onions, chopped
4 garlic cloves, diced
100g frozen sliced peppers

800g tomato base sauce
(page 167) or 2 x 400g tin
chopped tomatoes

Spaghetti, to serve

Add all the ingredients except the tomato base sauce or tinned tomatoes and spaghetti into a large freezer bag and seal well.

Freeze until the night before you want to eat it and defrost overnight in the fridge.

Drop the bag's contents along with the tomato base sauce or tinned tomatoes into the slow cooker.

Cook for 4–6 hours on high or 8–10 hours on low.

If you've made up the full batch, put half of the mixture in a freezer bag and freeze for later in the month.

Serve the other half with freshly made spaghetti.

HONEY SOY CHICKEN

This drop bag chicken dish saves on time but doesn't scrimp on flavour.

Serves 4

2 chicken breasts, diced
1 onion, diced
2 garlic cloves, crushed
170g honey
170ml soy sauce

85g ketchup
1 tbsp vegetable oil
¼ tsp red chili flakes

Noodles, to serve

Add all ingredients, apart from the noodles, to a freezer bag, seal well and place in the freezer.

Freeze until the night before you want to eat it and defrost overnight in the fridge.

Empty the bag into the slow cooker and cook for 4–6 hours on high or 8–10 hours on low.

Serve with plain noodles.

CHICKEN KORMA

All of the taste, not too many calories and a huge time-saving twist on a classic!

Serves 4

2 chicken breasts, diced
1 onion, diced
2 tbsp korma paste
1 tbsp creamed coconut
1l chicken stock

200g frozen cauliflower
200g frozen broccoli

Rice, to serve

Put all ingredients, except the stock, frozen veg and rice, in a freezer bag and freeze until the night before you want to cook.

Defrost overnight in the fridge and then drop it into the slow cooker, add the stock, and cook for 4–6 hours on high or 8–10 hours on low.

Add the frozen veg in 10 mins before it's finished, to cook.

If the sauce is too runny you can thicken it with 1 tbsp of cornflour mixed with 2 tablespoons of cold water.

Serve with rice.

SWEET PEACH CHICKEN

When I first found a recipe putting together chicken, ginger and peach I was intrigued! I don't know why these flavours work together but they do! So of course I adapted the recipe (simplified it and made it cheaper) and now it's one of my favourites!

Serves 4

2 chicken breasts, chopped
1 x 400g tin peach slices
2 peppers, chopped
1 red onion, sliced
2 tbsp brown sugar

4 tbsp soy sauce
1 tbsp ginger, grated
1 tsp black pepper

Rice, to serve

Put all the ingredients (including the peach juice), except for the rice, in a freezer bag and freeze until the night before you want to cook it.

Defrost overnight in the fridge.

Drop in the slow cooker and cook for 4–6 hours on high or 8–10 hours on low.

Serve with rice.

HARLEQUIN CHICKEN

You have to try this. The colours of the peppers give this dish its name.
Simple and delicious.

2 chicken breasts, diced
1 onion, chopped

3 peppers
(1 red, 1 yellow, 1 green)

400g tomato base sauce
(page 167) or 1 x 400g tin
chopped tomatoes

2 tbsp fresh parsley

3 tsp tarragon

2 tbsp lemon juice

2 tsp garlic powder

Rice, to serve

Add everything to a large freezer bag, apart from the rice, and pop it in the freezer.

Defrost in the fridge the night before using it, then add to a slow cooker.

Cook on high for 4–6 hours or 8–10 hours on low.

Serve with rice.

FAKEAWAYS

CHICKEN FRIED RICE

This is quick, easy and an absolute bargain. If you're following the 8 week plan, you'll have chicken left over from your Sunday roast chicken (page 88) to use in this. The rice is bulk-bought and, when combined with the frozen veg, means this dish only costs £1. I like to cook the rice the night before as it won't clump as much. Remember the safety guidelines on reheating rice – when you cook it initially, cool it as quickly as possible and, when reheating, make sure it is piping hot all the way through. You can also use this recipe to make egg fried rice – just leave out the chicken!

Serves 4

1 tbsp cooking oil

300g cooked and cooled rice
(day-old is best)

2 tbsp soy sauce

100g leftover cooked chicken

4 spring onions, sliced

100g frozen peas, defrosted

1 egg, beaten

Heat the oil in a wok or a large pan.

Add the rice, tossing it about to break up any clumps.

Add the soy sauce, cooked chicken, spring onion and peas and stir for 5 minutes until cooked through.

Once the veg is cooked, push the rice to one side of the wok. Add the egg and whisk until almost scrambled then quickly stir through the rice.

Mix thoroughly and serve.

CHICKEN CHOW MEIN

This recipe really does taste like the real thing. It takes far less time to cook than waiting for a delivery and it's a lot cheaper! When working on this recipe, I had to be inventive. Did you know it's five times more expensive to buy branded plain noodles in the world food aisle in most supermarkets than own-brand instant ones? Just throw away the horrid sachets that come with them and use the noodles. In 10 minutes you'll have takeaway-style chow mein that is as good as the real deal!

Serves 4

1 chicken breast, sliced
1 tsp Chinese 5 spice
2 tbsp cooking oil
1 tsp chilli sauce

2 nests egg noodles
200g frozen peppers
4 spring onions, sliced
1 tbsp soy sauce

Marinate the chicken in the 5 spice, 1 tablespoon of the oil and chilli sauce while you prep everything else.

Bring a pan of water to the boil, add the noodles and cook per packet instructions – if you use instant noodles like I do, make sure you DON'T add the flavouring packet!

Drain the noodles and drizzle over ½ tablespoon of oil. Toss well.

Place a wok or large frying pan over a high heat and add the remaining oil. Fry the chicken for 5 minutes, stirring to prevent it from sticking too much.

Add the veg and cook for a further 3 minutes, continuing to stir.

Add the soy sauce and fry for another 2–3 minutes tossing everything about well.

Finally, add the noodles and mix everything together before serving up.

'MAKE-YOUR-OWN' PIZZA NIGHT

When it comes to pizza bases, I've found that making them from scratch ends up being particularly expensive and no matter what I've tried, buying base mix has always worked out cheaper. When it comes to the toppings though, this is the perfect opportunity to use every scrap of leftover food in the fridge. Whether it's some shredded chicken, a handful of sweetcorn, leftover grated cheese, or tomato base sauce, there's no need to waste when you can simply chuck it on a pizza. These are always great fun for the kids, who love to get creative with their pizza toppings.

Serves 4	

Pizza base mix
(enough for 2 pizzas)

6 tbsp tomato base sauce
(page 167) or ½ x 400g tin
chopped tomatoes,
blitzed until smooth

Leftover meat
50g leftover veg
100g cheese, grated

Wedges, to serve
(page 176)

Preheat the oven to 200°C/Fan 180°C/Gas 6 and grease two baking trays.

Make up your pizza bases following the instructions on the packet.

Once rolled out and ready, spread a little tomato base sauce or blitzed tinned tomatoes over the pizza bases, and then add your meat and veg.

Sprinkle over the grated cheese.

Cook in the oven for 10 minutes or until crisp and bubbling.

For a true 'fakeaway' feel, I serve the pizza with corn on the cob and potato wedges. You can cook the potato wedges in the oven with your pizza so it all comes out ready to eat at the same time!

SOUTHERN FRIED CHICKEN

I'll be honest, this recipe is probably one of the longer ones in this book but I promise it's worth it. I am not usually that kind of cook – my whole mantra is to look at any recipe and ask 'how can I make it easier?' With this one the answer is you can't really but it's so good, and once you've made it, everyone will be begging you to make it again. It's even better than takeaway and once you have the herbs and spices in the cupboard they will last for AGES.

Serves 4

SPICE MIX:
2 tbsp paprika
4 tsp onion powder
2 tsp chilli powder
2 tsp black pepper
1 tsp celery salt
1 tsp dried sage
1 tsp garlic powder
1 tsp dried oregano
1 tsp allspice
1 tbsp dried basil
2 tbsp coarse sea salt

330g plain flour
2 tbsp sugar
1 egg, beaten
900g chicken thighs, bone in and skin on
Cooking oil, for frying

Make the spice mix by combining all the ingredients together in a bowl.

Add the flour and sugar to your spice mix, and combine well.

Put your beaten egg in a bowl, and dip each chicken piece into the egg then coat it in the spice mix. Set aside on a plate and repeat with the remaining chicken pieces.

Once all your chicken is coated, shake off the excess spice mix and you're ready to fry.

Heat enough oil in a pan to shallow fry the chicken, and fry batches over a medium heat for about 15–20 minutes, turning them so that they cook evenly.

Once they're cooked through and are a deep golden colour, place on kitchen paper.

Serve with salad and corn on the cob.

Make a double batch of the spice mix and store it in a tightly sealed jar. Next time you make this, it'll be MUCH quicker!

CRISPY CHICKEN NUGGETS & STRAWBERRY MILKSHAKE

Who doesn't love chicken nuggets? In my opinion, the best way to have them is with twice-cooked chips (page 175) and a strawberry milkshake!

> **Serves 4**

NUGGETS:
1 egg, beaten
100ml cold water
120g flour
2 tsp salt
1 tsp onion powder
¼ tsp black pepper
¼ tsp garlic powder
2 chicken breasts
4 tbsp cooking oil, for frying

MILKSHAKE:
250g frozen strawberries
100g yoghurt, frozen (page 188)
500ml milk
1 tbsp sugar, honey or sweetener
1 tsp vanilla essence

In a bowl, mix the egg with the water and stir.

Combine the dry ingredients in a freezer bag.

Place the chicken breasts on a chopping board and cover with cling film – so that bits of chicken don't go flying everywhere in the next step!

Bash the chicken fillets with a rolling pin until about ½ cm thick, then cut into bite-sized chunks.

Add the chicken to the freezer bag of flour and seasoning, seal it and shake it all about to coat all the pieces.

Remove the chicken from the bag and dunk them in the egg mixture, then pop them back into the dry mix.

Add the oil to a pan or wok and place over a medium heat. Fry the chicken for 10–12 minutes, turning to make sure they cook evenly.

Once they're cooked through and are a deep golden colour, place on kitchen paper.

Prepare your milkshake by blitzing everything together in a blender or food processor. Serve ice cold with your chicken nuggets and twice-cooked chips.

CRISPY CHILLI CHICKEN

This tastes very authentic and is one of my favourites! I've given a method for frying and baking the chicken, so do whatever works best for you and accompany with your favourite stir-fry veg.

Serves 4

25g flour

1 tsp garlic powder

1 tsp chilli powder

2 chicken breasts, thinly sliced

5 tbsp cooking oil if frying, or a couple of pumps of cooking oil spray if baking

Selection of vegetables for stir-frying

Cooked noodles

Spring onions, sliced

SAUCE:

120ml water

2 tbsp rice wine vinegar

1 tsp garlic, minced

1 tsp ginger, minced

2 tsp tomato purée

1 red chilli, chopped, or ½ tsp chilli flakes

1 tbsp honey or sweetener

Mix the flour, garlic powder and chilli powder together in a large bowl then toss in the chicken and coat thoroughly.

To fry:
Heat 4 tablespoons of the oil in a wok or pan over a medium heat, then add the coated chicken. Fry until crispy.

To bake:
Preheat the oven to 200°C/Fan 180°C/Gas 6. Prepare a baking tray by spraying it with cooking oil. Spread the coated chicken out on the tray, toss and spray again, then bake until crispy, about 20 minutes.

To make the sauce, put all the ingredients into a pan over medium heat, and stir. Bring it to the boil then turn the heat down to low and let it simmer for 10 minutes. Turn off the heat and leave the sauce to cool.

While your sauce is cooling, add 1 tablespoon of oil to a pan and stir-fry the vegetables over a high heat for 5 minutes, stirring or tossing them so they don't stick.

Add the noodles to heat through, stirring well.

Add half of the sauce and all of the chicken and give everything another stir to make sure it's mixed thoroughly.

Serve topped with spring onions and the rest of the sauce on the side.

CHICKEN KEBABS

These are great if you're having a bit of a gathering at home. People are always impressed! You will need either wooden or metal skewers for this recipe. You can use whatever veg your family like.

Serves 4

¼ bunch of fresh coriander
2 handfuls of fresh mint
2 garlic cloves
1 thumb-sized piece of ginger
2 tbsp salt
Pinch of black pepper
1 tbsp turmeric
2 tbsp cooking oil
200g Greek yoghurt (page 188)
4 chicken breasts, cut into large chunks
1 red cabbage
Mixed vegetables

DRESSING:
Juice of ½ a lemon
50ml olive oil or rapeseed oil
Salt & pepper, to taste

GARLIC MAYO:
5 tbsp mayonnaise
1–2 garlic cloves, minced
2 drops white wine vinegar
Pittas or wraps, to serve

If using wooden skewers soak them for at least 20 minutes before putting under the grill or BBQ.

Put the coriander, mint, garlic, ginger, 1 tablespoon of salt, pepper, turmeric and oil into a large bowl and blitz with a hand blender.

Add in the yoghurt and mix well.

Add the chicken, cover, and put in the fridge to marinate for a couple of hours while you prepare the sides.

Remove the core from the cabbage and thinly slice the rest.

Put the cabbage in a sieve and pour over 1 tablespoon of salt. Leave it to drain and dry over the sink for about half an hour.

Combine the ingredients for the dressing in a bowl, then add in the cabbage and mix well.

Mix the mayonnaise with the garlic in a separate bowl, adding the white wine vinegar to loosen it, then set aside for later.

Preheat the grill or BBQ.

Thread the chicken and veg onto the skewers and cook for about 20 minutes, turning so all sides are cooked through.

Serve with warmed pittas or wraps, tossing on the red cabbage and plenty of garlic mayo

FISH & CHIPS WITH MUSHY PEAS

This is a perfect Friday dinner based on a chip shop favourite. A top tip here to get it tasting like the takeaway version is to dry the fish before battering it, otherwise the batter just slides off and turns to mush.

Serves 4

240g plain flour
3½ tbsp baking powder
Salt and pepper to season
270ml ice-cold water
Oil, for deep frying

450g frozen fish fillets
200g frozen peas

Twice-cooked chips, to serve
(page 175)

Preheat the oven to 180°C/Fan 160°C/Gas 5.

Put the flour and baking powder in a large bowl and season with salt and pepper.

Add the water and mix to form a batter. You'll need to keep the batter cold and use it within 20 minutes.

Heat the oil in a large saucepan or deep fat fryer to 160°C.

Cut the fish into portions and then pat dry with kitchen paper and season with a little more salt and pepper.

Dip two pieces of fish in the batter.

Fry for about 8 minutes until golden brown. It's good to fry two pieces at a time, so they don't crowd each other out and reduce the oil temperature.

Remove from the oil and drain on kitchen paper, then put them in the oven to cook through and keep warm while you cook the other pieces.

To make mushy peas boil the frozen peas and once they are cooked, mash them down (or leave as they are if you don't fancy them mushed!)

Serve up the fish and mushy peas with twice-cooked chips.

SWEET & STICKY CHINESE BEEF

This is a great dish if you want to make something a bit different. Don't worry if you don't have any cooked roast beef, as you can use stir-fry beef strips too by cooking them first. You can also use pretty much any veg you like.

Serves 4

3 tbsp cornflour

2 tsp Chinese five spice

350g cooked roast beef, sliced into strips, or stir-fry beef strips

4 tbsp oil, for frying

2 garlic cloves, finely chopped

2cm piece of ginger, finely chopped

1 red pepper, sliced

1 carrot, thinly sliced into julienne strips

A couple of handfuls of mange tout, diagonally sliced

SAUCE:

4 tbsp white wine vinegar or rice wine vinegar

2 tbsp sweet chilli sauce

2 tbsp tomato ketchup

1 tbsp soy sauce

Long grain rice, to serve

Mix together the cornflour and Chinese five spice.

Toss in the sliced beef and mix it all around to coat well.

Heat the oil in a wok or large frying pan.

Fry the coated beef in batches until crispy and drain on kitchen paper.

Fry the garlic, ginger and the rest of the veg for about 3 minutes in the same pan (mind you don't burn the garlic).

Mix the sauce ingredients together, drain the oil from the pan and add in the sauce to cook for another 2 minutes.

Add the beef to the pan and cook for another 3 minutes.

Add a little water to the wok to loosen the sauce.

Serve with long grain rice.

DONER STYLE KEBAB

A much, much healthier version of what becomes everyone's guilty pleasure after a few drinks on a night out! Put this in the slow cooker before you head out for the evening and come back home without having to stop at the kebab shop. It'll save time, money and your waistband!

Serves 4

SPICE MIX:
1½ tsp cayenne pepper
1 tsp salt
1 tsp black pepper
1½ tsp garlic powder
1 tsp dried oregano
1 tsp dried mixed herbs

500g minced lamb
Pitta bread, to serve
Salad leaves, sliced cucumber and corn cobettes, to serve
Chilli sauce, to serve

Mix all the spice ingredients together.

Put the mince into a bowl and add the spices. Mix really well into the meat – get your hands into it and really work it all together. You'll probably have to get quite heavy-handed.

Once the spices and mince are well mixed, form it into a loaf shape.

Place in the slow cooker and cook for 4–6 hours on high or 8–10 hours on low.

Once cooked wrap the meat tightly in foil for at least 10 minutes before slicing.

Serve in pitta bread with the lettuce and cucumber and a drizzle of chilli sauce. Corn cobbettes are great on the side.

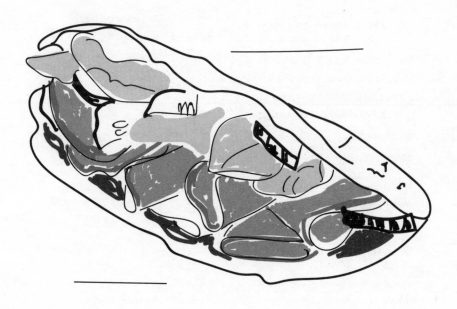

SWEET TREATS

HONEYCOMB

I guarantee you that kids will absolutely LOVE helping with this recipe! Not only is this stuff dynamite, making it is also like a science experiment!

> **Serves 4**

100g caster sugar
4 tbsp golden syrup

1 ½ tsp bicarbonate of soda

Line a large dish or baking tray, or you can use a large piece of tin foil – you'll need it ready, this recipe waits for no one!

Put the sugar and syrup into a saucepan and stir to mix before you put it on the heat. You won't want to stir it once it's on the hob!

Put the pan on the medium heat. Watch it closely as it becomes gooey, starts to bubble and turns the colour of maple syrup.

Take off the heat and quickly whisk in the bicarbonate of soda (you'll love this bit as it kind of looks like a volcano).

Pour it out immediately onto the lined dish or foil and wait for it to cool.

When set, break it into shards and it's ready to eat! Alternatively, for extra indulgence, you can cover it with melted chocolate or go at it with a rolling pin to crush it into a crumbly topping which you can then use to sprinkle over ice cream.

Honeycomb keeps for ages, so if you have any spare, just pop them into a freezer bag and seal.

MINI JAM TARTS

I always make these when I have some pastry left over from cutting pie crusts out. Though I have been known to make a full batch! I like to use my homemade jam in these, but any kind will do.

Makes 24

Shortcrust pastry
(page 196)

Jam or curd of your choice
(page 190)

Preheat the oven to 200°C/Fan 180°C/Gas 6 and grease 2 bun tins.

Roll the pastry out onto a floured surface.

Cut out 24 discs using a cookie cutter or, if you don't have a cookie cutter, use a glass or a mug.

Lay the discs out on the prepared tins.

Put a teaspoon of jam or curd onto each disc.

Bake on the top shelf of your oven for about 10–15 minutes, until the pastry is golden, then cool on a wire rack.

The jam will be like molten lava so try to resist eating one straight away!

MINI JAM DOUGHNUTS

Who doesn't like a jam doughnut? No, I didn't think so! But just in case, you can fill them with whatever you want – make them custard doughnuts, chocolate doughnuts or even apple or banana doughnuts – all doughnuts are made equal in my eyes! These are easy, cheap and so much fun to make. You'll need a syringe to put the filling inside, and a thermometer to make sure the temperature is right.

Serves 6

150g plain flour
2 tsp baking powder
50g caster sugar
Pinch of cinnamon
1 large egg

2 tbsp milk, to bind
Cooking oil, to fry
Sugar, for dusting
Seed-free jam

In a large bowl, add the first four ingredients and stir together to mix.

Make a well in the centre of the ingredients and add in the egg and milk to bind to make a thick cake-like batter.

Heat the oil to 170°C (about 5cm of oil in a wok is enough).

If you don't have a thermometer, try dropping a tiny bit of the batter in and when it bubbles, the oil is ready.

Once the oil is very hot, add the batter in tablespoon-sized amounts. Make sure not to overload the pan as your doughnuts will increase in size as they cook.

Turn the doughnuts regularly and cook for about 3 minutes until they are lightly browned.

Once cooked, drain on kitchen paper and roll in sugar.

Use a syringe to pipe jam (or whatever other filling you've chosen) into the doughnuts – kids love this bit!

If you don't have a syringe, try a piping bag (or a sandwich bag with one corner snipped) and nozzle.

SLOW COOKER CHOCOLATE CAKE

I know you're looking at this and thinking, chocolate cake? In a slow cooker?! It's a very different cake from most and to be perfectly honest I have no idea why it works, I just know that it does. Give it a go – but I mean it when I say below, don't stir it!

Serves 8

CAKE:
130g plain flour
150g white sugar
3 tbsp cocoa powder
2 tsp baking powder
¼ tbsp salt
125ml milk
75g butter
2 tsp vanilla essence

TOPPING:
100g caster sugar
100g soft brown sugar
25g cocoa powder
350ml hot water

To make the cake, combine the dry ingredients in a bowl, then make a well in the centre.

Add the milk, butter and vanilla essence to the well, and whisk until the mixture is smooth.

Pour the batter into the slow cooker.

To make the topping, mix the sugars and cocoa powder together in a bowl and sprinkle evenly over the top of the cake batter.

Pour the hot water evenly over the mix – and don't stir! I know it doesn't make sense, I know you'll want to, but trust me, don't stir!

Put the lid on and cook on high for about 4 hours.

Serve straight out of the slow cooker with ice cream or custard.

TOASTED HAZELNUT BALLS

You won't need three guesses to work out what these are a homemade version of! We often make them at Christmas to give as gifts, but they are perfect little balls of energy to have whenever you need a boost or if you just have a hankering for something sweet.

Makes 30

200g whole hazelnuts
200g hazelnut spread

120g chocolate wafers, finely chopped
400g milk chocolate, broken up

Toast the hazelnuts in a dry pan over medium-high heat until they just start releasing their oils. Keep a close eye on them as when they go, they go quickly and you don't want anything to burn!

Once toasted, keep 30 whole nuts to one side. Blitz the rest in a food processor.

In a small bowl, mix the hazelnut spread and chopped hazelnuts until well combined.

Pop in the freezer for about an hour until the mixture is stiff enough to be rolled into balls. Once it's hard enough to mould, take a teaspoon of the mixture and work it around a whole hazelnut so you have a hazelnut centre with a chocolatey outside.

Next, roll the ball in the chopped wafers and put back in the freezer. Repeat with the remaining ingredients.

Melt the milk chocolate in a glass or Pyrex bowl over a pan of simmering water until all the chocolate is melted. It should be smooth and glossy.

Dip each ball into the melted chocolate, coating them as evenly as you can.

Sprinkle over more wafers or chopped hazelnuts then keep in the fridge until ready to eat.

COOKIES & CREAM FUDGE

This one is an absolute classic that is so moreish I have to give it away or else I'd eat it all myself! If I have some of my easy cookies (page 162) stashed away, I use that in the fudge instead of using shop-bought.

125g butter
200g sugar
1 tbsp liquid glucose
1 x 397g tin condensed milk

200g white chocolate, grated
7 chocolate chip cookies, broken into quarters

Grease and line a 23 x 23cm baking tin.

Put the butter, sugar, liquid glucose and condensed milk into a heavy-based saucepan and heat gently to melt, stirring frequently to prevent sticking.

When the mixture has darkened in colour and thickened (this is likely to take around 30 minutes), add in the grated chocolate and stir until melted – it only takes a minute – then stir through the biscuits.

Pour the mixture into the prepared tin, score squares into the surface make cutting easier and put the tin in the fridge to chill overnight.

The following day, cut the fudge into squares. Store in the fridge, but remove about 10 minutes before eating.

PEANUT BUTTER CUPS

My homage to a favourite treat! We've found these make great gifts and to be honest, I can't think of a more iconic duo than peanut butter and chocolate.

Makes 48

BASE:
50g soft dark brown sugar
200g icing sugar
50g softened butter
200g smooth peanut butter

FILLING:
50g crunchy peanut butter
200g milk chocolate, broken up
100g dark chocolate, broken up
A mix of peanuts and hazelnuts

Put all the ingredients for the base into a food processor and pulse until it's a sandy in texture.

On a baking tray, lay out 48 mini muffin cases.

Add one teaspoon of the base mix to each case and press it down firmly, covering the bottom of the cases evenly which creates the base for each cup.

Add ½ teaspoon of the crunchy peanut butter to each case, trying to spread it evenly to cover the base.

Set a heatproof bowl over a pan of simmering water.
Add the milk and dark chocolate and melt gently. Keep stirring as it melts to prevent the chocolate from sticking to the bowl!

Add a layer of melted chocolate to each case.

Decorate each peanut butter cup with chopped or whole nuts and leave to set in the fridge.

LORNA'S EASY COOKIES

I've yet to meet anyone who doesn't like these simple, adaptable and tasty cookies. Oh, and there's a reason they're called easy! They're usually gobbled up quickly, but if I have any left, I like to use them in my cookies & cream fudge (page 160).

Makes 12 filled and 12 regular

225g margarine
110g sugar
280g plain flour

A filling of your choice: jam, peanut butter or curd
50g chocolate chips

Preheat the oven to 180°C/Fan 160°C/Gas 4 and line a baking tray.

Cream the margarine in a large bowl. Add the sugar and whisk until light and fluffy.

Add the flour and mix well before forming the mixture into a dough.

Halve the dough and use one half to roll out 12 balls.

Place on the baking tray and flatten with a fork. Use your finger to push a dent into each cookie.

Add ½ teaspoon of your chosen filling into each hole.

Bake for 12–15 minutes then cool on a rack.

With the remaining dough, make your regular chocolate chip cookies by mixing in the chocolate chips and rolling into 12 balls.

Place on a baking tray and flatten with a fork, as before.

Bake for 12–15 minutes then cool on a rack.

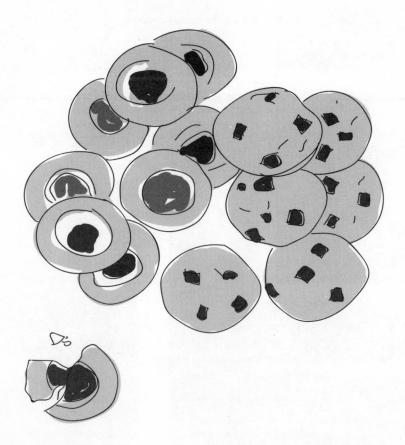

BASICS

SAUCES

These sauces are delicious, easy to make and versatile, and are used in many of the recipes in this book. If you look at most brand-name sauces, you'll see they almost all have something extra: garlic, bacon or sweet pepper in a tomato sauce or cheese, parsley or peppercorns in a béchamel. You can jazz up these base sauces too by adding extras when reheating, and you'll have a whole range of fancy sauces at your fingertips!

TOMATO BASE SAUCE

This sauce has transformed my cooking. Packed full of veg – you can use practically ANY veg to make it, fresh or frozen – and blitzed once cooked, you can use this in place of tomato sauce or even tinned tomatoes. I make this in a huge batch and freeze it in portions, defrosting as needed. My kids love it, and they have no idea how healthy it is!

Makes 3 litres

1 tbsp veg oil
2 onions, diced finely
100g frozen spinach
50g frozen carrots
200g frozen casserole veg
50g frozen cabbage

2 x 400g tin tomatoes
2 tbsp tomato purée
2 tbsp Worcester sauce
1 tbsp mixed herbs
1.5l stock

Heat a very large saucepan, add the oil and fry the onion for a few minutes, then chuck everything else into the pot and bring to the boil.

Reduce the heat and leave to simmer for 45 minutes stirring occasionally until it is thick and looks glossy.

Leave the sauce to cool, then blitz it in a food processor in batches or with a hand blender until smooth.

Have a taste and, if needed, add a teaspoon or two of sugar to neutralise the tomatoes. Remember, brand-name sauce often has up to 6 teaspoons of sugar in one jar, so yours is still MUCH healthier.

WHITE BASE SAUCE

I use this white base sauce, or béchamel, for all my creamy sauces – cheese sauce, parsley sauce, peppercorn sauce – you name it!

30g butter   500ml milk
30g flour

In a saucepan, melt the butter over a medium heat then stir in the flour. It will clump together but don't worry, it's supposed to look like that!

Cook for 2 minutes and then stir in the milk. Whisk continually until it starts to thicken.

If you're adding any extra ingredients such as cheese, parsley or peppercorns, add them now, then reduce the heat and simmer for 2 minutes.

FYF BURGER SAUCE

Don't let the name fool you. This one is easy to make, super tasty and you don't
have to limit it to burgers either!

115g mayonnaise
1 tbsp mustard
2 pickled gherkins, diced
1 tbsp vinegar

½ tsp garlic powder
½ tsp onion powder
½ tsp paprika

Add all the ingredients to a bowl and mix.

Then use your hand blender or food processor to blitz everything
together.

Serve with burgers, or anything else really (it even goes well with
kebabs). It's the easiest sauce you'll ever make.

EGGS

Let's talk eggs. On a budget, buying free-range might not be an option but if you can afford it, I do recommend doing so. Eggs are a great staple because they're filling and versatile, whether they're boiled, poached, fried, scrambled or made into an omelette.

OMELETTE

An omelette is a great way to use up fridge gravel and the results are always delicious!

Serves 4

1 tbsp oil

2 onions, diced

6 eggs, beaten

Cheese, grated

Leftover cooked meat and veg

Preheat the grill to medium

Heat the oil in an oven-safe frying pan over a medium heat and fry the onion until it has softened.

Add in your leftover meat and veg to heat.

Pour in the eggs and add the cheese, then stir the egg mixture as if you were making scrambled eggs, until it's almost cooked.

Cook for another few minutes without stirring so the bottom sets, then put your frying pan under the grill until the top has set.

POTATOES

My nana always used to say, 'if you've got potatoes in, you've got the makings of a meal.' If you can, it's always a good idea to shop around at the market or a local farm where you can buy a sack of potatoes. If you're worried about using up a full sack, consider sharing with family or friends. Make sure to store your potatoes in a dark, dry place in a paper or hessian bag (plastic makes them sweat and go mouldy). Don't store them near onions, as they will go bad more quickly. If you pop an apple in with them, it prevents sprouting.

Chips, wedges, jacket potatoes and roasties can all be prepped ahead and frozen to save time on a weeknight. Mash can be cooked and frozen, just don't add any butter or milk until you reheat it. A good rule of thumb is that anything you buy frozen can also be frozen at home!

SLOW COOKER JACKET POTATOES

These are so easy to prep and freeze ahead of time. Prick the potatoes with a fork then rub a little oil into the skins. Place the potatoes in the slow cooker and cook for 8–10 hours on low, or 4–6 hours on high. Once they have cooked and cooled, you can wrap them in foil or plastic and freeze until needed. I've included two of my favourite toppings here.

TUNA MAYO

1 tin of tuna, drained

200g frozen sweetcorn

2 tbsp mayonnaise

Defrost your sweetcorn then mix everything in a large bowl and serve over your potato.

BEANS AND CHEESE

1 x 400g tin baked beans

50g cheese, grated

Simply pop the toppings on when you heat up your potatoes so that the cheese is melty and delicious.

FONDANT POTATOES

500g potatoes, peeled and cut
into chunks

100ml vegetable stock

Preheat the oven to 200°C/Fan 180°C/Gas 6.

Bring a pan of water to the boil, then add the potatoes and parboil for 5 minutes.

Drain and put them in a roasting dish, then pour over the stock and bake until all the liquid has been absorbed and they are soft. This will take around 25 minutes.

TWICE-COOKED CHIPS

500g potatoes,
peeled and cut into chips

500ml oil
Salt, to serve

Place the raw chips into a saucepan or colander and sit them under cold running water until the water runs clear. You can leave in cold water until needed, just drain and dry the potatoes thoroughly when you're ready to cook them.

Heat the oil in a saucepan or deep fryer to 130°C – don't leave the pan!

Put the chips into the hot oil and fry for about 10 minutes until softened but not coloured then remove the chips from the oil and drain on kitchen paper.

Increase the heat of the oil to 190°C then add the chips back in and fry for another 3–5 minutes until golden. Drain on kitchen paper as before then season with a little salt and they're ready!

POTATO WEDGES

500g potatoes, cut into wedges
1 tbsp cooking oil

1 tsp Cajun spices

Preheat the oven to 200°C/Fan 180°C/Gas 6.

Bring a pan of water to the boil, then add the wedges and parboil for 5 minutes.

Drain, then spread the wedges onto a baking tray. Pour over the oil and Cajun spices (or salt and pepper if you don't like spice) and toss well until all the wedges are coated.

Bake in the oven for 20 minutes, turning occasionally to ensure they are golden all over.

ROAST POTATOES

2 tbsp cooking oil

500g potatoes, peeled
and cut into chunks

Preheat the oven to 220°C/Fan 200°C/Gas 7.

Put the oil onto a baking tray and put it in the hot oven.

While the oil heats, bring a pan of water to the boil, add the potatoes
and parboil for 10 minutes.

Drain and put the potatoes onto the baking tray and toss well. Bake
for 30 minutes until tender and golden.

ROOT MASH

150g frozen Swede

4 large carrots,
peeled and sliced

2 parsnips, peeled and sliced

30g butter

Salt and pepper

Put all the veg in a large saucepan and cover with water. Bring to the boil and then reduce the heat and simmer for 20 minutes, or until the swede is cooked through.

Drain the veg then return to the pan.

Add the butter then blitz with a hand blender or mash. Season with salt and pepper.

POTATO / VEGETABLE PEEL CRISPS

You may have heard that a lot of the nutrients in potatoes are found just under the skin so we often end up throwing away the best bit, but did you know you can make crisps from them? You can also use parsnip or carrot peel, and season with chilli flakes, cumin or paprika.

Potato peel
2 tbsp cooking oil

Salt and pepper, to taste
Seasoning (optional)

Preheat the oven to 200°C/Fan 180°C/Gas 6

Put the peel on a baking tray and drizzle over the oil, then sprinkle over the salt, pepper and seasoning. Get your hands dirty, mixing it all in to make sure the peels are covered.

Bake in the oven for 8–10 minutes.

HOMEMADE STOCK

Stock can be made easily and cheaply at home from stuff you would usually throw away, like a chicken carcass, the water you cooked a gammon joint in or the vegetable peelings from dinner. It's tasty and reduces waste!

HOMEMADE STOCK

Stock can be made easily and cheaply at home from stuff you would usually throw away, like a chicken carcass, the water you cooked a gammon joint in or the vegetable peelings from dinner. It's tasty and reduces waste!

POULTRY

Place the poultry bones into a large saucepan or slow cooker. Cover with water and cook for a few hours on the stove top or overnight in the slow cooker. Strain and discard the bones and you have a lovely stock. Just don't mistakenly strain over the sink and watch your hard work go down the plug! So many people have said they've done this without thinking!

VEGETABLE

You do need quite a lot of peelings to make this stock full of flavour, so I usually keep a bag of vegetable peelings in the freezer that I add to until full. Follow the same method as for the poultry stock. Potato peelings don't work well for this.

MEAT

When you've cooked meat in water, such as a ham hock, strain and save the juices to use as stock or to make gravy.

TRADITIONAL GRAVY

No roast dinner is complete without gravy and this recipe saves you from spending on shop-bought, pre-made gravy or granules. Plus, it will remind you of the roast dinners your nana used to make.

Juices from a joint of meat
30g plain flour

500ml stock
(use appropriate stock for the meat you've cooked)
Salt and pepper, to taste

Once your meat has been removed from the roasting tin, pour the juices from the tin into a jug and allow to settle.

Put the roasting tin you used on the hob over a medium heat. When the juices in your jug cool, the fat will float to the top. Skim off the fat with a spoon and add it to the roasting tin along with the flour.

Cook for 1 minute then gradually stir in the meat juices and stock. Use a wooden spoon to swirl the liquid around the pan to lift any baked-on scraps.

Bring to the boil and simmer for 10 minutes, stirring continually to make sure it stays smooth and lump-free. Season to taste and serve in a gravy boat or jug.

Basics

PORRIDGE – 3 WAYS

Porridge is a staple and there are so many ways you can make it. Use a slow cooker for busy weekdays or make a porridge pot if you need porridge to go. Cooking times might vary depending on what kinds of oats you're using.

TRADITIONAL POT METHOD

Serves 4

150g porridge oats
1l milk or water or a mixture
of both

100g frozen fruit,
to serve (optional)
Toppings

Put the oats in a medium-sized saucepan over a medium heat and stir in the liquid.

Bring to the boil stirring frequently, then reduce to simmer for 4 minutes.

If you're using frozen fruit, add and cook for a further minute. Then serve, topped with your favourite porridge toppings.

SLOW COOKER

150g porridge oats
500ml milk
500ml water

Toppings
(fruit, honey, cinnamon etc.)

Put the oats, milk and water in a heatproof bowl and sit it in a few centimetres of water in the slow cooker overnight on low (you can put everything directly into the slow cooker, but this way stops it from going too dry).

Add your toppings in the morning before serving.

PORRIDGE POT

Serves 1

50g porridge oats

1 tbsp milk powder

2 tbsp dried fruit (optional)

350ml boiling water

Add the dry ingredients to a small tub or jar with a tight-fitting lid. When you're ready to eat, just pour in the water and stir thoroughly. Leave to stand for a couple of minutes, then stir again before eating.

HOMEMADE YOGHURT

If you spend a lot on yoghurt, this recipe will change your life.
Lots of people don't know this, but yoghurt makes more yoghurt – sort of like
live yeast and bread – so you can have an endless supply of yoghurt, as long as
you always remember to keep a portion of your culture back for the next batch.
All you need is a good old-fashioned Thermos and a thermometer!

350g milk (UHT
or fresh)
40g powdered milk

1½ tbsp natural
yoghurt (live)

Pour the milk and powdered milk into a saucepan and use a small
whisk to dissolve the powdered milk.

Place a thermometer in the saucepan and heat it to 82°C, then let it
cool down to 46°C (this takes about 10 minutes).

Meanwhile, prepare your flask. Fill with boiling water and screw
the lid on. This will sterilise it and offer the milk a nice warm
environment.

Once the milk has reached 46°C, whisk in the yoghurt. Empty out
the water from the flask and replace it with the milk-yoghurt mixture.
Screw on the lid tightly and leave overnight (not in the fridge).

If you want a thick Greek-style yoghurt line a colander or sieve with a
muslin cloth and strain the yoghurt through.

FLAVOURING YOGHURT

Have you ever looked at how much sugar is in flavoured yoghurts, especially the ones aimed at kids? Not only are they high in sugar, they're also pretty pricey!

Once you've made natural yoghurt (or even if you buy plain yoghurt, which is often cheaper than flavoured), you can flavour it however you like, and skip the artificial colours, E-numbers
and high sugar content of the shop-bought variety.

For fruit flavours I use jam or frozen fruit as it's super-soft when defrosted and you can just mash it up and stir through. For vanilla yoghurt, simply add vanilla essence or extract to taste. For honey yoghurt, just add honey. Chocolate yoghurt? Add chocolate spread. You see where I'm going with this? It's not rocket science!

JAM

Making your own jam is a great way to use up any excess fruit you may have. Taking the kids fruit-picking is loads of fun and if you live near woods or hedgerows you can often find fruits like blackberries in abundance. Just remember to ask the landowner's permission first! You can usually find soft fruits in the reduced sections in supermarkets during the summer months, and you can, of course, use frozen fruit instead. The method depends on the fruit you use, and I've given a few options below. Simply follow the method given, then move to the final step on the next page.

BLACKBERRY JAM

Makes 3 x 300ml jars

900g blackberries
50ml water

1½ tbsp lemon juice
900g granulated sugar

Place the blackberries, water and lemon juice into a large saucepan and bring to the boil. Lower the heat and simmer for 15 minutes until the fruit is soft. Tip in the sugar and stir over a very low heat until dissolved. Raise the heat and leave at a full rolling boil for 10–12 minutes.

STRAWBERRY JAM

Makes 3 x 300ml jars

900g strawberries   900g granulated sugar
3 tbsp lemon juice

Place the strawberries and lemon juice into a large saucepan
and bring to the boil. Lower the heat and simmer for 5 minutes
until the fruit is soft. Tip in the sugar and stir over a very low heat
until dissolved. Raise the heat and leave at a full rolling boil for
20–25 minutes.

PLUM JAM

900g plums, halved
and destoned

150ml water
900g granulated sugar

Place the plums and water into a large saucepan and bring to the
boil. Lower the heat and simmer for 30–40 minutes until the fruit is
soft. Tip in the sugar and stir over a very low heat until dissolved.
Raise the heat and leave at a full rolling boil for 10 minutes.

RASPBERRY JAM

Makes 3 x 300ml jars

900g raspberries   900g sugar

Place the raspberries into a large saucepan and bring to the boil (adding no liquid). Lower the heat and simmer for 2 minutes. Tip in the sugar and stir over a very low heat until dissolved. Raise the heat and leave at a full rolling boil for 5 minutes.

Final Step: When the jam begins to set, remove it from the heat and skim off the excess scum. Stir in a knob of butter (this helps to dissolve any remaining scum) then leave for about 15 minutes to settle. Pour into sterilised jars (pour boiling water into them then drain), label, seal and enjoy at your leisure!

DRYING FRUIT AT HOME

Dried fruit is expensive, but it's also super-tasty and great to have on hand, so here's how to dry your own. I recommend making large batches because if you're running the oven for a long time, you might as well. If you're lucky enough to live somewhere sunny you can also dry fruit outside in the sunshine!

Ripe fruit

Lemon juice solution (equal parts water and lemon juice)

Choose ripe or just overly-ripe fruit and give them a good wash in cold water. Remove any blemishes or stones, then cut or slice the fruit into similar sized chunks.

Make up a solution of equal parts lemon juice and water and soak the fruit in it for 10 minutes, then dry carefully on kitchen paper.

Preheat the oven to the lowest temperature it has and lay your fruit out on a baking tray so they don't touch. I like them curly, but if you don't want them to curl, place another baking tray on top.

Bake for 6–8 hours rotating the trays every couple of hours if you can. Remove from the oven when ready (it should be leathery but still pliable).

Transfer the fruit into glass or plastic containers (you can sterilise them first with boiling water, but make sure they're completely dry). Leave the lids off for a couple of days to allow any remaining moisture to disappear, then seal and you are good to go! They'll keep for up to 10 months.

SHORTCRUST PASTRY

Pre-made pastry is really expensive compared to the cost of the ingredients. It might take you a couple of attempts to get it right, but once you've mastered it you will never look back. You can make a large quantity, portion it up and freeze to use as needed. This recipe makes enough for a 23cm pie base and crust.

400g plain flour
Pinch of salt

200g butter,
chilled and cubed
3-4 tbsp cold water,
to mix

Mix the flour and salt, then add the butter using your fingers to rub it in until it resembles breadcrumbs. You can do this in a food processor if you have one.

Add the cold water gradually, bringing the mix together into a dough. Wrap in cling film and place in the fridge for at least 30 minutes before freezing or using. When you need to use it, you can defrost overnight in the fridge, or at room temperature for about 3 hours

WRAPS / FLATBREADS

You'll save yourself a fortune by making these yourself. Don't worry if they don't look as uniform as shop-bought ones, they'll taste just as good, if not better, and you will eventually become an expert at getting the shape right!

Makes 6 wraps or 4 flatbreads

300g self-raising flour
½ tbsp vegetable oil
Pinch of salt

Cold water, to bind
Dried seasoning (optional)

Add the flour, oil, salt and seasoning (if using) to a bowl, then add in a little water until you have a sticky dough.

Tip out onto a well-floured surface. For flatbreads, hand press until they are about ½ cm thick.

For wraps, use a rolling pin to flatten, using plenty of flour so they don't stick.

Place a dry frying pan over a high heat and cook on both sides – wraps will need 1 minute per side, flatbreads will need 3 minutes per side.

INDEX

ACKNOWLEDGEMENTS

Firstly, I'd like to say a massive thanks to everyone who has been involved in the FYF Facebook page for the last 5 years! To all the admins who have contributed at different times but especially Eve and Penn – you helped me build an amazing online community. And to the members of that community, special thanks to each and every one of you. Without your feedback, engagement and encouragement, none of this would have happened. Thank you for helping us reach the people who need us most – without your shares and recommendations they wouldn't know we exist!

To Gary Hunter, without whom I would never have made the giant leap from a mum who ran a Facebook page to a businesswoman and author! You inspired the confidence in me to achieve this momentous goal!

To Lauren Lunn Farrow for introducing me to Carly Cook who has been an absolute godsend! Carly has guided me through this entire process with grace, patience and understanding. Believe me when I say she has talked me off the ledge many a time! Don't let anyone ever tell you writing a book is easy – it isn't!

To the crew back in the office in Seaham. You guys are amazing! Thank you for welcoming me, helping me out, teaching me and always making me laugh! But I especially must thank the following: the all-knowing Warrick, who hates being nice to me but is always there when I need to vent or if I need advice (which is ALL the time). You are a giant among men and I'm grateful to know you! The lovely and very talented writer Megan who has such a sunny disposition she always makes me smile! And Sam, the business brain who makes sure the i's are dotted and the t's are crossed and who, in my opinion, definitely should have won Bake Off! You were robbed Sam!

To all the wonderful people at Orion. Anna Valentine, my publisher, who believed in this book from the start. To Lucie, Anna, and Sophie for all your hard work in putting this book together, correcting my spelling mistakes, making sure everything was perfect and turning an idea into a beautiful book!

First published in Great Britain in 2020 by Seven Dials
an imprint of The Orion Publishing Group Ltd
Carmelite House, 50 Victoria Embankment
London, EC4Y 0DZ
An Hachette UK Company

10 9 8 7 6 5 4 3 2

A CIP catalogue record for this book is
available from the British Library.

ISBN (Mass Market Paperback) 978 1 8418 8449 3

Publisher: Anna Valentine
Art Direction and Design: Lucie Stericker
Editor: Shyam Kumar

Printed in Great Britain

www.orionbooks.co.uk